THE DYING AND
LIVING LORD

THE DYING AND
LIVING LORD

HELMUT GOLLWITZER

SCM PRESS LTD
56 BLOOMSBURY STREET
LONDON

TRANSLATED FROM THE GERMAN
Jesu Tod Und Auferstehung
(4TH EDITION, CHRISTIAN KAISER VERLAG, MUNICH, 1956)
BY OLIVE WYON
FIRST PUBLISHED 1960
© SCM PRESS LTD 1960

PRINTED IN GREAT BRITAIN BY
EAST MIDLAND PRINTING CO LTD
BURY ST EDMUNDS

CONTENTS

TRANSLATOR'S PREFACE

These meditations on the passion and resurrection of our Lord, now translated into English, had their origin in Dr Gollwitzer's work in Berlin during the years 1939 and 1940, when he was successor to Dr Martin Nicmöller as pastor of the congregation of the Confessing Church at Dahlem. In those fateful years Dr Gollwitzer drew strength for his congregation from St Luke's Gospel, expounding it Sunday by Sunday, often in the context of Holy Communion. Not long after the end of this course of sermons he was expelled from Berlin by the Nazis. Later he served as a medical orderly in the German army on the Eastern front. His experiences after the war in captivity in Russia were the subject of a well-known book, translated into English as *Unwilling Journey* in 1953. Now Professor of Theology at the University of Berlin, he has revised and expanded his last Dahlem sermons, believing that their message is still the only true source of peace and strength in our age of anxiety.

In this translation, the quotations from the Bible are taken from the Revised Standard Version, except for the Psalms, which are quoted from the Anglican Book of Common Prayer.

OLIVE WYON

I

Luke 22.39-46

And He came out, and went, as was His custom, to the Mount of Olives; and the disciples followed Him. And when He came to the place He said to them, 'Pray that you may not enter into temptation.' And He withdrew from them about a stone's throw, and knelt down and prayed, 'Father, if Thou art willing, remove this cup from Me; nevertheless, not My will, but Thine, be done.' And there appeared to Him an angel from heaven, strengthening Him. And being in an agony He prayed more earnestly; and His sweat became like great drops of blood falling down upon the ground. And when He rose from prayer, He came to the disciples and found them sleeping for sorrow, and He said to them, 'Why do you sleep? Rise and pray that you may not enter into temptation.'

THIS story is beyond all human understanding. If we want to join the disciples of Jesus, and to listen once more to the Passion story during these weeks of Lent, we must be prepared to hear nothing but the record of events which transcend the grasp of human reason. In short, this is a story which, although it uses human language, can do no more than hint at its meaning. Even if we have entered deeply into the Passion narrative —even if we have identified ourselves with it to such an extent that we have felt something of the overwhelming sorrow and sadness which gripped the disciples with an almost paralysing effect on that night—even if at the same time we are aware of the secret thread of joy which runs through our Passion hymns, because while they re-live the last terrible events of Holy Week they write from the standpoint of the Resurrection —even then, we shall only have *begun* to have a glimpse of the meaning of these events. For the Passion story is beyond our understanding.

Excepting the Christmas story, perhaps there is nothing with which we can compare this story of that night in Gethsemane. For here all human language fails. It is as though the narrator, once he has uttered the words which hint at the meaning of this story, falls silent—and then—after an endless moment of pregnant silence—and only then—goes on with his story. For instance, we may well ask : what does the word 'temptation' mean here? or the word 'sorrow', as applied to the disciples? We are told nothing about it. The evangelist is silent; for here no human being *can* say anything. Finally, we cannot help asking ourselves : what sort of prayer is this, which the disciples may have overheard as they were on the point of falling asleep—or perhaps they only caught the words of the central utterance through the heaviness of their unnatural sleep? Why was there this terrible agony in prayer, causing the Son to sweat blood? We cannot even begin to understand the meaning of this prayer unless we have some glimmering of an understanding of the relation between the Father and the Son which lies behind it. Unless we are aware of this relationship and its significance—even if only in a very dim, imperfect manner—we shall get involved in lesser questions which only lead to fruitless discussion, e.g. how did the disciples know anything about this prayer at all? The real question is—why did Jesus have to wrestle so much in His prayer? Was He afraid of death? We can think of so many striking examples of people who met death so bravely and calmly. We remember that His disciples themselves died quite differently, when they suffered martyrdom for His sake.

Here is no question of the fear of death, in the usual human sense of the words. For why did Jesus now suddenly begin to shiver and shake, when He had previously spoken about God with such truth and power, when He had proclaimed the Kingdom of God and its eternal character with such force, and indeed had imparted this power so impressively at the Last Supper? 'He began to be greatly distressed and troubled,' says Mark the Evangelist. The Greek text uses a terrible word : 'He began to despair.' This is the expression of an unspeakable horror—of an infinite suffering. It seems to go far beyond anything that anyone on this earth could ever experience, something that goes further than any suffering which had ever been endured upon this earth before. Something quite different seems to be happening. It seems to be a horror in presence of the strange plan and decree of God Himself. The Evangelists Matthew and Mark, in their account of this event, express this 'horror' very strongly. Mark says that Jesus fell down upon the ground, and Matthew adds that He fell upon His face. Luke seems to have toned this down when he says that Jesus 'knelt down' upon the ground, but the way in which the other two Evangelists write about it seems to suggest something which far transcends ordinary human experience.

It was a terrible conflict! Why? Against whom or what was Jesus fighting? Against the force of temptation? But that is not the point here. He warns the *disciples* against falling into temptation, but He Himself is not fighting against temptations of the flesh, against anxiety, or the fear of suffering; He is waging a far more terrible battle. Martin Luther translates : 'He was wrestling with death.' The Greek word *agonia*, which is used here, is the word for the final struggle with death. But this seems very strange; for this suggests that He was fighting with death hours before He was put to death. This suggests that it was not really Pilate and the soldiers and the Jews who put Him to death. Who was it then?—'Father, if Thou art willing, remove this cup from Me!' Here is a Man whom *the Father* is putting to death. In the Marcan story Jesus appeals to the Almighty Power of the Father. Almost commandingly He says: 'Abba, Father, all things are possible to Thee; remove this cup from Me.' In the Gospel of Luke this prayer

11

becomes a quite humble petition: 'Father, if it be in accordance with Thy plan, let this cup pass Me by.' It is a conflict of the Father with the Son, and of the Son with the Father. In the Lucan account, in particular, it is clear that this conflict was not due to any spirit of rebellion, or refusal to do the will of God, on the part of Jesus Himself; rather, it suggests a conflict *within* God Himself. It seems to mean that Jesus is asking the Father whether this 'way' is necessary. And it suggests the answer: 'Yes, this "way" must be trodden to the very end; it cannot be altered.'

Here, as in the Christmas story, all our 'conceptions of God' break down. Our Passion hymns are impregnated with the consciousness of the great price God has paid to redeem us; of the fact that it is *He* who bears the cost. This seems to be a contradiction; for Almighty God has no difficulty in exercising His will; He need not make any special effort to render it effective. The fact that *here* God treads the path of painful effort and suffering is something which is so great, so inexplicable, that it lies beyond the range of human reason. It has cost Him a terrible conflict, and infinite suffering; it has cost Him the anguish of being plunged into all the suffering of the whole human race. When we hear the words of the Gospel of John: 'God so loved the world that He gave His only begotten Son', *here* we see what that means. 'He that spared not His own Son'! This means that Jesus is the Son of God in the sense that He really shares the lot of humanity as a whole. Here indeed we see that not only did He take a real share in the suffering of humanity, but that here all human suffering reaches its climax; all is gathered up in Him. For He is now offering a strange prayer—one that had never before been prayed upon this earth, nor will ever be offered here again. In this prayer He includes us all, and in this prayer we are all saved. And He who prays like this is now preparing Himself to take upon His own shoulders all that lies before us: death, and more than death, for He who could not live without God will have to endure the extreme agony of desolation, of rejection. 'Christ redeemed us from the curse of the law, having become a curse for us; for it is written, *Cursed is everyone that hangeth on a tree*' (Gal. 3.13).

God's Son plunges into those depths and takes upon Himself the extreme horror of human existence, which would have awaited each one of us, when we were brought face to face with God. Calvin has said, rightly, that this hour in Gethsemane was our Lord's descent into hell. He has gone through hell, 'into the extreme of misery, in order that I might not die'.

That is what it has cost God to redeem us; and we live on this today. Anyone who today is afraid of death may be sure of this: in the night of Gethsemane. Jesus too felt this pain with you. If you are troubled and perplexed today, because God has permitted something terrible to come upon you, you may be sure of this: that Jesus of Nazareth, in the night of Gethsemane, has gone through this too; He has borne with you and for you this experience of temptation and conflict. And 'because He Himself has suffered and been tempted, He is able to help those who are tempted' (Heb. 2.18). But there is more in it than this! If you are passing through the still more bitter experience, not only of suffering or sorrow, but of the sense of your own guilt—if you are suffering not only from mental distress but from the sense of your own sin, fearing not only death but hell, you may be sure of this: that Jesus Christ has already been through hell; He has taken the terror of it upon Himself, and has delivered you from its destruction. 'Thou hast led captivity captive' (Psalm 68.18). And now we are no longer cast out into the outer darkness of despair. Now we have nothing more to fear, for we have been redeemed. He has fought the fight—that is what it has cost God to redeem us.

It was not a conflict with doubt, but it was a conflict within faith. It was not the conflict of One who was in the very least concerned about Himself; it was the conflict of One who was fighting God's battle—fighting hard that the will of God might be *done*. He was not asking to be spared any suffering for Him-

13

self, but whether it was possible that *God* might be spared from paying the utmost cost. The fact that the People of God should reject and kill the Lord's Anointed would constitute a terrible breach in God's relation with His Chosen People upon earth. In this act, God's humanity would be alienated from God. What Jesus was asking (in His prayer) was this : whether this final breakdown could be avoided? whether the human race could be preserved from committing this final sin? 'Can it be possible,' he seems to say, 'that God has given man the potentiality, the power, and the opportunity, to reject Him, in such a way that man may prove unworthy of salvation, and may therefore be in danger of losing it? Is it not His mission, with one final mighty effort, to strive against this, to prevent it from happening?' It was not for His own sake, but for the sake of *God*, that the cup was so bitter for Jesus. When He asks 'if it be possible', He does not mean that God's power is limited and that God Himself is subject to a higher necessity, but He is inquiring into God's purpose—and that is why in Luke's Gospel the question of Jesus is rightly expressed : 'Wilt Thou?' Jesus is suffering not only from the crime of man, but from God's purpose. In Gethsemane, 'although He was a Son, He learned obedience through what He suffered' (Heb. 5.8). In Gethsemane the God-Man, the obedient Man, struggles, learns, and prays, and surrenders not only His human will, but also His religious will, His divine will, wholly to the will of God, does nothing in His own interest, but offers everything—not only His own life, but also the cause of God, to God Himself. For this reason He receives from God Himself the strength He needs to tread this path : 'There appeared to Him an angel from heaven, strengthening Him.'

Now what is the 'temptation' of which Jesus is thinking, which includes a great concern for His disciples? He does not say what it is that He sees threatening us. It may be that He saw the temptation to which Peter almost fell a prey, with the best intentions in the world—the temptation to give his help to the divine cause by drawing the sword in defence of his Lord. It may be that He saw Peter's temptation to save himself trouble by denials. It may be that He saw the disciples' temptation to answer thoughts of hatred with hatred. Possibly He saw temptation arising for the disciples from this very conflict within God Himself; it was a temptation to be shaken by this impotence of God. 'Blessed is he who takes no offence at Me.' One thing, however, is certain : that He sees us threatened on every side, and that at a moment when He Himself is going into the fiercest temptation, He is not anxious about Himself in the very least, but He is wholly concerned for His disciples, and both before and after this incident He says to them nothing but : 'Pray that you may not enter into temptation.'

So we go into Passiontide and Holy Week as human beings who are surrounded by temptation. None of us have any right to think that it is only outward danger which gives us so much cause for anxiety nowadays. Our souls are still more terribly menaced, and the souls of very many people, who fall into great misery and suffering through the guilt and sin which have been heaped upon them, and which we all should really fear. That is the real injury, the real menace in all dangers.[1] Jesus' conflict in Gethsemane is like a strong protection and guard. We continually fall into the sleep of indifference and carelessness, and perhaps, when we have gone through still worse experiences, we fall into the sleep of paralysing sadness like the disciples. But this Protector holds us firmly in His grasp and drives away the temptation which threatens us; for He is with us. So we go into Passiontide, from the very beginning, as persons whom God has comforted, since God has not spared His only Son. 'Because He Himself has suffered and been tempted, He is able to help those who are tempted' (Heb. 2.18). 'For God so loved the world that He gave His only Son, that whoever believes in Him should not perish but have eternal life.' (John 3.16).

[1] One of a number of oblique references to the Hitler *régime* (*Translator*).

II

Luke 22.47-53

While He was still speaking, there came a crowd, and the man called Judas, one of the twelve, was leading them. He drew near to Jesus to kiss Him; but Jesus said to him, 'Judas, would you betray the Son of Man with a kiss?' And when those who were about Him saw what would follow, they said, 'Lord, shall we strike with the sword?' And one of them struck the slave of the high priest and cut off his right ear. But Jesus said 'No more of this!' And He touched his ear and healed him. Then Jesus said to the chief priests and captains of the temple and elders who had come out against him, 'Have you come out as against a robber, with swords and clubs? When I was with you day after day in the temple, you did not lay hands on Me. But this is your hour, and the power of darkness.'

THESE are the last words of Jesus which the disciples heard from His own lips before His death. The three sentences are addressed to the traitor, to themselves, the disciples, and to His persecutors. And then He goes away from them. Peter sees Him once more from a distance, it is true, and Jesus looks at him—and then—they do not see Him again until He is on the Cross. Previously He had warned them with the words, 'Rise and pray, that you may not enter into temptation!' And then come the words, 'While He was still speaking, there came a crowd'. Evidently this means that with the crowd, the *temptation* of which He had just been speaking had already arrived. Now it has come upon them. And the three sentences

16

in this passage were spoken to meet this test. In this decisive hour He thinks first of these men in danger : of the temptation which assails them now, when they see Him betrayed by one of their own circle, of the temptation which assails them when He prevents them from defending Him, of the temptation which assails them when the power of His enemies seems to be victorious. St Mark tells the story in such a way as to suggest that between the kiss of Judas and the blow with the sword Jesus stood quite still, in profound silence. Hence when St Luke adds some words to this incident it does not mean that his account contradicts the Marcan narrative, but rather that these words of Jesus come out of a profound silence, and indeed that they express the meaning of this silence. It is the *silence of the Victor*; that is why these words contain no complaint and no accusation. Jesus is about to taste the bitterest experiences of His whole life, concentrated in a few hours. But, even before this happens, the bitterness has been wholly overcome. The words which now come to us as a help in our temptations proceed from the mouth of One who has already wholly conquered the temptation, One who has no complaints to make, no arguments, in self-defence. All His thoughts are wholly one with the Will of His Father; no longer has He any desires of His own; He has no wishes for Himself at all, because His whole will and desire is bent on carrying out the mission with which He has been entrusted. That is why these words also convey a great sense of *freedom*. They are the words of One who, outwardly, in the bitterest experience, evidently has no thought of Himself at all; He is wholly concerned with the needs of others, both in His thoughts and His words. Thus at the very moment when everyone else is full of anxiety about himself and has no thoughts to spare for his neighbour, Jesus speaks in a spirit of utter freedom, showing that His love embraces them all : the traitor, His enemies, His friends, His would-be champions—all alike.

If Judas had only had 'ears to hear'—if only he had not been so obsessed with his own plans—indeed, if only he had not already surrendered himself so fully to the Satanic power—when Jesus spoke to him he might have realised that even now the Son of Man was calling him—Judas—seeking 'to save' him. That is why Jesus uses the word 'Son of Man' in this question. 'Judas, would you betray the *Son of Man* with a kiss?' The question is intended to remind him : 'See, it is the *Son of Man* who is speaking to you, He who has come "to seek and to save", and He is asking this question with no other purpose than to bring you to your senses.' It really means: 'Do you realise *Whom* you are betraying? The *Son of Man*—and that means, according to the prophetic words (of Daniel 7): The Hope of God upon earth, the Help of God upon earth, the culmination of all your own hopes. For have you indeed any other hope than this, apart from the Son of Man?'

When Judas realised what he had done, it was inevitable that he should hang himself. He had betrayed his Master—and the realisation drove him to despair, for he had no idea of the love he had injured, no idea that this love was still seeking him, even in the midst of the darkness of betrayal.

A great many attempts have been made to explain the enigma of the motives of Judas. The Bible gives us no explanation—probably because it does not matter what his particular considerations and motives were. All that really matters is the fact that, whatever his motives may have been, he was a man who had struck out on a line for himself—a line which ended in the fact that he, a disciple of Jesus, 'one of the twelve', St Luke adds with horror, took the side of the world against the Gospel. So it came about that at the end of his self-chosen path he threw up his apostolic mission altogether, and instead, showed the world how to get rid of the Gospel. In so doing, he also helped to betray Christ and His Church into the hands of their enemies, so that they became the 'prisoners' of the world—no longer a danger to the world, because they had been 'handed over' to the world. The horror of this treachery was intensified by the fact that Judas committed this crime under a pretence of love and loyalty, as if he were really concerned for the Gospel, for Christ and His Church.

The Church is continually confronted by the terrible possibility that this kind of treachery can still take place within it—that even a man who holds office in the Church may commit this crime. No period in church history has been free from such incidents. The evangelists were probably right in suggesting that whatever other motives may have been at work, at least money did play some part. Either the desire for money or anxiety about money : 'What shall we eat and what shall we drink?' Again and again this leads a man to decide for the world, and to betray Christ with a kiss. But when this happens, the Son of Man, even at the moment when He is being betrayed, still seeks the 'lost sheep', the traitor, and asks him : 'Do you know Whom you are betraying?'

We can, I hope, now understand why 'those who were about Him' wanted to intervene by force. *Those who were about Him*—henceforward, this is how Luke describes the company of the disciples. The fact that he does not use the word 'disciple' is probably because, by the act of betrayal, the circle has been broken at its heart; it was only after the Resurrection, when Christ gave it a new meaning, that the circle could be re-formed. Indeed, we cannot help understanding why this group wanted to intervene with the sword. When things like this are happening, how can we stand by and do nothing? That is why Jesus seems not to want to blame them; He simply tells them to put away the sword and says : 'No more of this!' When He says this, at the very moment when He is being handed over into the hands of His enemies, He is the Master of the situation. He stops the fight which is about to break out; He heals the injured man, and in so doing works His last healing miracle. This shows that He does not want any blood to be shed on His account; for He has not come in order to increase the suffering of humanity, but to heal it. That is why, even at the last moment, He heals, and thus shows us that the only weapon of His Church is to care for all, even for our enemies, and to suffer martyrdom. Truly where the Church has understood this, there she has been strengthened to overcome. Everyone who wants to be on the side of Jesus, and to stand up for Him, is unfit for the struggle so long as he thinks that by force and resistance he can carry on the fight.

Those who want to be on the side of Jesus, and to fight for Him, must listen to this commanding word. It means first that they must be wholly ready for suffering, and thus expose themselves to the conflict into which they are sent. In this conflict, under no circumstances have they any right to try to spare themselves suffering. The battle waged by the disciple of Christ is not concerned with evading suffering, but with outspoken witness even in the midst of suffering. Secondly, a Christian, like his Lord, may under no circumstances treat his opponents as his enemies. The war which is waged by a disciple of Christ is always a war *against* himself, and *for* the enemies of the Gospel. By the way in which he meets their hostility he must make it clear, even to them, that he is waging this warfare on their behalf. No one can prepare himself for this better than by listening to the words of warning spoken by Christ, as they are recorded in the Johannine tradition: 'Put your sword into its sheath!' (John 18.11). In the last resort, it means this: you who are going forth to fight for Christ must first of all become silent and learn. Only when you are involved in the fight against yourself will you be able to fight with others in the way in which you fight against yourself. Thus you must be a person who, through Jesus Christ, has become wholly one with the will of God. Then you will understand what Jesus meant about obedience to God when He said: 'No more of this!' Let them go on, for God conquers! Let them carry on, for here God's cause is being fought for! It is not a party matter, it is not the affair of a clique. Here stands the Son of God—not as the leader of a party against other parties; here we are *all* involved, for the reality of salvation for *all* men is at stake. Any one who grasps this with his whole heart and mind, and thus becomes one with the will of God, will truly become a disciple, and a champion of Jesus Christ upon earth.

Finally, Jesus speaks to His persecutors. He speaks in such a way as to reveal the lie which has brought them together. 'Have you come out as against a robber with swords and clubs?' Jesus means: 'Since you have come with such a purpose, you want to pretend that this is the arrest of a dangerous revolutionary.' From time immemorial, again and again, the war against the Gospel has been represented as a political conflict.[1] But Jesus shows up the deceit which lies behind this accusation. He seems to be saying: 'You know very well that I am no dangerous revolutionary, you know very well that this is a false suggestion, which you want to impress on others by your display of armed force. You know very well that it is not your responsibility to the state which drives you to proceed against Me. It is inner enmity, a profound hatred, which drives you to do away with Me, and makes you want to kill Me!'

Here again Jesus is speaking as the Lord. It is of His own free choice that He allows them to continue in their chosen line. 'This is your hour and the power of darkness.' The 'hour' at which God's salvation is accomplished upon earth is at the same time the hour when darkness seems triumphant. All through the Passion story it is suggested that this is the secret of the suffering of Christ: God conquers, and frees us from the darkness, by emptying the battlefield and giving Himself up to the power of his enemies. The darkness does not then prevail —it is *endured*, because it is leading to the fulfilment of the purpose of God. And this applies to every 'hour' since then in which the darkness appears to get the upper hand and to accomplish something. But there is no 'hour' when God forgets to rule, no hour in which His power is checked contrary to His will, no hour in which His power has reached its utmost limits and can extend no further. Whenever this seems to

[1] As by the Nazis at this time (*Translator*).

21

happen, God, in His sovereign wisdom, allows the darkness to remain, but He uses it for His purpose, and makes it part of His way of carrying out His plan for the world.

Thus no one can fight against this darkness in the right way unless he utterly surrenders himself to the will of God. We do not know the reason why this must be so. But we know the end, and we know the heart of God. The end is the Resurrection, the victory of God, and our salvation. The heart is the love of God for all men in the darkness. That is why Jesus says to the man who betrays Him, to those who try to defend Him, and to His persecutors: 'Whatever you may be today, and whatever you may become, a traitor, a champion, or a persecutor, whatever you may be, I am seeking you.' Jesus did not allow Himself to be frightened away by our sin—and that was the last thing He saw upon earth—from going into the darkness for our sakes. So every word which He still speaks in this last hour is a cry from the heart of that limitless, overwhelming mercy which is always seeking and finding us.

III

Luke 22.61-62

And the Lord turned and looked at Peter. And Peter remembered the word of the Lord, how He had said to him, 'Before the cock crows to-day, you will deny Me three times.' And he went out and wept bitterly.

I n these weeks, when the Church is specially remembering the Passion of Jesus, we have gone a certain way along the *Via Dolorosa*. We have accompanied Him a good long way; we have not refused to follow when we heard of His sufferings. We remained with Him, and went with Peter to the point where the Lord stood before the judgment seat. And yet in spite of this, nothing has really happened. Jesus of Nazareth, we would agree, is a unique figure, and His words are unforgettable; we admit that we also expect something from Him, and can attribute something in our own lives to His influence; all that is as it may be. And yet He only really enters our lives when we suddenly know what it is to stand with Peter and to weep bitterly. There are many Christians who observe Lent, Holy Week, Good Friday and Easter, and many who go to the Lord's Supper, but the Church of Jesus Christ exists in reality only where two or three people suddenly begin to 'weep bitterly'.

Why is Peter weeping? A man may often come near to weeping, in this world. We may feel like weeping over the

23

way in which God's wonderful creation has been spoilt, this world of which it was said: 'And God saw everything that he had made, and, behold, it was very good.' The beauty of the spring reminds us so forcibly of the original goodness of the creation. It cannot be explained away by us, or be an illusion. But we only need to open our newspaper and to read what men and women are making of this lovely world, to feel like weeping bitterly, even if we are fairly 'tough' and not given to tears. Why is Peter weeping? Is he weeping because the world, and humanity as a whole, is being defaced? Is he weeping over the wickedness of men, over their unbelief, their superficiality, the way they play on the edge of the abyss, their hard-heartedness and their icy coldness, their false morality? Or is he weeping over Jesus, and the evil fate which has overtaken Him? Is he weeping over the fact that the Man to Whom the people flocked, and Who helped everyone, now has to tread the despicable path of rejection, as if He were a criminal?

We may weep over such things to our heart's content. All that this really means is that we have a certain sensitivity for things as they are. The kind of person that the Bible calls the 'natural man' can do this quite well. *We* can do this too, and perhaps we think this is the right way to react to the Passion story. 'Peter wept bitterly,' but he did not weep over this or that or the other, nor over the world and humanity, nor even over Jesus: *he was weeping bitterly over himself*.

This also applies to the Christian Church. Indeed, without it there is no faith at all. But we do not weep like this unless we are treading the path which Peter trod at that moment. It is a path which is indescribably remote from the other; and it is one that none of us can tread of ourselves. Out there, in the Garden of Gethsemane, Peter was the champion of Jesus Christ; he was indignant at the treachery of Judas, angry about the behaviour of the soldiers and the temple-police, bitter about the hostility of the Pharisees, and ready to sacrifice himself and all he had. Then he drew his sword, and lashed

24

out: he was a man ready to confess his faith, and he thought that he would never allow himself to be separated from this Man, Jesus Christ. That is the sort of man he was out there on the hillside. He was a man who could weep bitterly over things which move many of us to tears in this world of ours, but he was not a man who wept bitterly over himself. Something else had to happen.

What had happened since then? He had denied his Master. And this denial consisted in the fact that he who was ready to cleave to his Lord—and that is why he went with Him—who was ready to stand up for Him—and that is why he drew his sword—that he, who had gone so far along this way, was tripped up in an insignificant conversation, in a small incident, in the presence of unimportant people: maidservants and gatekeepers and menservants. At first, all he did was to draw back a little way from this Man, Jesus of Nazareth, saying: 'Woman, I do not know him.' Perhaps he thought that this was not a 'denial'. A proper denial would be something so terrible. Surely, that was what the words of Christ had referred to, when He had said: 'Before the cock crows to-day you will deny Me three times'? But what Peter has just said is nothing of that order. Did he not feel courageous enough to stand up before the whole Council, and even before Pilate himself? Surely, he could not dream of denying all that had hitherto been sacred to him? And then, a little fear crept into his mind, and with the fear came also the excuse, needed in order to evade those questions. Perhaps he thought: 'Here it's hardly worth speaking out! Is it fitting to expose one's belief before these people? Ought I to throw pearls before swine? Have I got to tell everybody what I think?' Perhaps, too, there was a little shame in his heart. It was such a miserable situation. There was nothing romantic about it—nothing to make one feel that one even wanted to make a confession of faith in a Master who now looked so wretched, in a Master who had been so battered, as He had been dragged from pillar to post. And so Peter said: 'I do not know the Man.'

25

We sometimes think that we have plenty of courage, and that we are ready to say 'I am not ashamed of the Gospel of Christ!' and we really do not feel afraid, at least not to any great extent. But if this Man, carrying in His face and walk all the marks of the rough and cruel treatment He has received, were to come forth from the door and pass by, and were suddenly to look round—is there one of us who would not feel impelled to weep bitterly? Perhaps we have never denied Him. Perhaps on the contrary we have been rather eager to confess Him before men; possibly we have talked too much about it rather than too little. But even if we have had this amount of courage, it does not amount to much when Christ looks at us. Can we recall incidents when Jesus approached us in the person of some 'poor wretch'? 'He has no form or comeliness.' He is 'despised and rejected of men'. 'He comes to us in a poor fellow-man!' Is it not the case that Christ Himself has come to us in the shape of some poor or needy person—an outcast, or someone whom we find repulsive, someone indeed who may be rightly condemned—asking our help? Behind each of these people stands Christ Himself, expecting something from us: nothing less than a confession of faith! And then perhaps, too often, instead of making a confession of faith, from shyness, or perhaps simply out of laziness and indifference, we have joined in the usual talk about this person which amounts to saying, 'I do not know the man'. And then Christ looks at you—and you realise that this was not an indifferent little bit of by-play, that this person was not unimportant. This poor wretch had a right to be answered, for tacitly he asked you whether you too belonged to this Jesus of Nazareth. It was Christ who asked you in the person of this miserable man; and you withdrew from Christ, and put Him off with a brusque remark: 'I do not know the Man.'

The same applies to our attitude to the Church, the Church of the present day, with all its faults, surrounded as she is by many enemies. Here, too, it is with Christ Himself that we have to do. And whenever we have adopted an aloof attitude, in conversation, whether quiet or loud, at a greater or lesser distance from the Church in its hour of need and oppression—whenever we have made some carping criticism of the servants of the Church, but have refused to carry any responsibility ourselves, saying self-righteously 'I won't get involved in these questions . . . it's nothing to do with me!'—we have in effect said: 'I do not know the Man!' Whenever this happens it shows that we have failed to realise that this *does* concern us, that we are now going against our own inmost feelings and our knowledge of truth; we know that here we ought to confess that we have been led astray by fear of 'unpleasant-ness', that we have tried to throw dust in our own eyes by thinking: 'It doesn't seem worth making a protest at this point!'

So as we approach the Lord's Table today, we ought to know that we are exposing ourselves to the gaze of Jesus of Nazareth. It is He who now passes before us, and turns towards us, and *looks* at us. No human word could make us feel that this *look* strikes us like a flash of lightning. But God grant that it may strike us, in order that we may begin to weep bitterly. Then we shall have no time to think about all those other external things: the evil and stupidity and laziness and coldness of other people; the guilt of the Church and the nation; the suffering and dominion of death upon this earth. Henceforward we will only think about ourselves, and we will begin to weep bitterly over ourselves. For this 'look' of Christ is that of an innocent man who was put to death. As He passes before us on His path of sacrifice He is treading the way to execution which we should be treading ourselves. His look penetrates us, and each of us knows: 'It is I, it is I, who have to repent.' But he goes on His way and is nailed to the Cross, and we walk scot-free, while an innocent Man is put to death; and all we can find to say about Him is: 'I do not know the Man.'

And as His gaze pierces our souls, we see that He is the One

27

Who does nothing but good, from whom we have received nothing but good, Who was always ready to help, Whose hand was always open, Whose words were always loving, and to Whom none came and was ever turned away. This is the look of the great Benefactor Who has done everything for us—and now He stands there, and we perceive that all we could do in face of the words and death of the Christ Who became poor for our sakes, and to Whom we owe everything, is to say: 'I do not know the Man.'

This 'gaze' of Christ exposes everything. 'For the word of God is living and active, sharper than any two-edged sword, piercing to the division of soul and spirit, of joints and marrow, and discerning the thoughts and intentions of the heart' (Heb. 4.12). No pretence and no self-justification is now any use; nor does our previous fidelity help us either, nor all our good works. All we can hear are the words: 'I do not know the Man.'

'Weeping bitterly'—that is the Church of Jesus Christ. Only someone who has been pierced by this gaze of Christ, of the Christ who is on His way to the Cross, by the gaze of Christ Who hangs there for the whole world and sees us all, only he can understand why it is that there is so much talk of sin in the Church, and why our Passion hymns are so full of this bitter self-knowledge: 'It is I, it is I, who have to repent.' If we have not experienced this gaze, how can we understand these things? But when we are met by this look of Christ what *can* we do save weep bitterly?

But in saying this we must not forget that when Peter saw Jesus looking at him in this way it *reminded* him of something. 'And Peter remembered.' He remembered the words Jesus had spoken to him, and this increased his shame. One who has been ashamed of this Man, is now only ashamed of himself. Was he not told beforehand that this was what was going to happen? While Peter was still full of fight, and courage, and fidelity, Jesus had seen through him, and knew his weakness: 'Before the cock crows to-day you will deny Me three times.'

But in this book of Jesus which reminds Peter of all this, there is more than judgment. It is a look of mercy. By this glance of Jesus Peter is reminded that He, the Lord Whom he has denied, knew it all beforehand and had foretold it. And since He knew it beforehand, it did not prevent Him from treading this way for him. All this foreknowledge—'this man is going to deny Me, this man, at the moment when I have to go through the extreme of suffering, will say of Me "I don't know Him" '—this knowledge was already there in the mind of Jesus when He gave the Bread and the Wine to Peter at the Last Supper, and when He said: 'This is my Body, this is My Blood, given for you, poured out for you.'

So Christ does not reproach us by flinging back our own words at us, and He does not answer our denial by saying to the Father: 'I know not this man.' The law which threatened us has been broken: 'He who denies Me before men will be denied before the angels of God' (Luke 12.9). That does not happen, but a miracle takes place—*grace* happens. The wonder of all wonders is this, that *grace* breaks the iron law that the one who denies his Master will in time be denied by Him. *This* is what the gaze of Jesus means; this had already been proclaimed a few hours earlier in the first Eucharist; this is now confirmed when He does not allow this denial to hinder Him on his way to the Cross, but still goes on, into the cell, into the trial, to Golgotha.

So this 'bitter weeping' already contains the seed of consolation. Already it is not a hopeless weeping. It is sadness over oneself, it is true, but it is no longer the 'sadness unto death'; it is a godly sorrow. 'For godly grief produces a repentance that leads to salvation and brings no regret' (II Cor. 7.10). Easter is already within it; here Jesus of Nazareth gives the Eucharist to Peter, although an hour or two later he will deny Him. Easter is already there—for the man who weeps bitterly when Christ looks at him, the man who does not try to escape but looks at Him and does not assert his pride, the man who lets himself be guided, the man who says: 'Yes, it is

29

true that I am the one who denied Him three times. In this denial I see what I am! I am guilty! But I will stay with Thee, O cast me not out!'

And then He comes and hands you the Bread and the Wine, and says to all of us poor people: 'Because I live, you will live also.'

IV

Luke 22.63-71

Now the men who were holding Jesus mocked Him and beat Him; they also blindfolded Him and asked Him, 'Prophesy! Who is it that struck you?' And they spoke many other words against Him, reviling Him.

When day came, the assembly of the elders of the people gathered together, both chief priests and scribes; and they led Him away to their council, and they said, 'If you are the Christ, tell us.' But He said to them, 'If I tell you, you will not believe; and if I ask you, you will not answer. But from now on the Son of Man shall be seated at the right hand of the power of God.' And they all said, 'Are you the Son of God, then?' And He said to them, 'You say that I am.' And they said, 'What further testimony do we need? We have heard it ourselves from His own lips.'

'The men who were holding Jesus'—can this be true? Can anyone 'hold' God? Is not God the One who rules the clouds, the winds and the waves, the One who dwells in light inaccessible, whom none can approach? Did not this very Jesus, by the power of God, still the raging of the wind and the waves? Did He not conquer death at Nain, and at the grave of Lazarus? Did He not forgive sins, cast out demons? And now, can human beings 'hold' Him? In these words do we not feel something of the horror which runs through the whole of the Passion Story?

In the story of Jesus the reality of God had become visible;

31   C

it reached a height of reality, which, as the miracles of Jesus show, outstripped all other realities, and made them meaningless. And now, this reality, of its own will, takes a line which allows it to fall into the hands of men, to be powerless, at their mercy. God's help is rejected, and beaten by men—that is Christ's way of the Cross.

Those who beat Him then, and those who do the same today, are beating themselves. Those who mock Him, are mocking themselves. For the Man Whom they are 'holding' with their rough hands, the One Whom they have been beating, was Himself their own life; and when they spit upon Him they are insulting the One Who was and is our only hope. Again and again we are horrified, as we read and ponder the Passion story, to think that here we could be so *mad* as to act against ourselves—that we men are so perverted that we do all we can to insult our true life, our real hope, and then to beat, and spit upon, and revile it.

Those men thought that they had Him in their power. All who since that day have ventured to 'hold' Christ by their own power have thought the same. He Himself said plainly to one of them: 'You would have no power over Me unless it had been given you from above' (John 1.11). But they knew nothing of this; perhaps they felt rather relieved that they had been able to beat this prisoner without suffering any ill effects themselves. Possibly before this they had been slightly afraid of this Man. They had heard so much about Him that they felt He must be able to do all kinds of things; and this made them feel rather frightened about what might happen to them if they laid hands upon Him. But with every blow they became surer, every blow strengthened their feeling: 'He can't *do* anything!' The very thing that caused such sorrow to men of vision— 'O great and terrible sorrow, God Himself is dead! We hoped that He was the One to redeem Israel—but He is dead'—is, for those who are thus blinded, their great triumph: 'God is dead! He cannot do anything.'

His disciples saw this, and could not grasp it. Of course

they must have been dimly aware that this impotence of God could not be the whole truth. But they did not understand to where it would lead, and that is why they all forsook Him and fled. They avoided the scene of shame and hopelessness—but Jesus remained. He remained there, in deep silence. Even the Evangelist breaks off his narrative and leaves Him alone, while he goes on to describe the incidents which took place the following morning: 'and when day came . . .' The hours that lie between are shrouded in mysterious silence. They were hours of profound loneliness, hours too of secret communion between the Father, reigning in eternity, the Father who had sent Him, and the Son who here lies on the cold damp flagstones of the underground cell, bound with cords, battered and bleeding, deserted by all. During those hours He endured those sufferings which were, ultimately, to bring us all 'the benefits of His Passion'. The Father confirms the mission He has given to the Son . . . and the Son confirms, to the Father, His readiness to carry it out; the conflict in Gethsemane lies behind Him. 'In the world you have tribulation, but be of good cheer, I have overcome the world.' Now he no longer *asks* for anything, not even that the cup may pass Him by; from His tortured body there comes His complete surrender to the Father's will.

And when day came, He stood before His judges. Those who were to try Him were the official representatives of the Church, of the chosen People of God upon earth; they spoke for those who had been called out of the world in order to expect Him, and to receive Him as their King. Above them, on the walls of the hall in which they were gathered, was inscribed in golden letters the great confession of faith recited of the People of Israel, by young and old as frequently as we use the Lord's Prayer. 'Hear, O Israel: the Lord our God is One Lord' (Deut. 6.4). It was there, above them, as a warning and a reminder. They themselves, dignified, respected, blameless men, sat round in a semicircle as the custom was, in order that when the sentence was pronounced each could

33

look the other in the face. On this occasion the sentence had already long been decided in their own hearts. The accused had Himself evoked it from them, and with each of His deeds, in every word and every miracle, the sentence of death was more deeply engraved upon their hearts, and their rejection had become more firmly fixed than ever : 'We will not tolerate this man!' Directly after the raising of Lazarus, as we learn from the Apostle John, the religious leaders had decided to put Him to death. There may have been some who, as John tells us, were on the side of Jesus; in any case they did not dare to confess Him now, 'for fear of the Jews'. So as Jesus went to His death, He had to bear what so many others who have been accused have experienced, that judges do not give a true judgment, that they consent to a wrong sentence—for fear of this or that person.

Since they already knew what the sentence would be, they were in a hurry to get it over. Jesus was arrested about midnight; by the next afternoon He was already hanging on the Cross. Since it was laid down in their law that before a death sentence could be passed there had to be two sittings of the Council, these sittings took place within a short time of one another. But it was also laid down that no execution might take place during the Feast of the Passover, and they were not afraid to ignore this law—since the command to eliminate a blasphemer rendered the other commandments null and void, and 'after all, it would be the heathen Romans who would actually carry it out!' There Jesus stood between two great candles, as the question was put to Him : 'If you are the Christ, tell us!' When they put this question, they had no idea of the greatness of this hour, the crisis of this question.

Here it is not the Christ Who is asking *us*, His disciples, human beings, whether we know Who He is. Here it is not Christ Who is confronting us with a demand, but it is we who confront *Him*. Caiaphas, who was speaking in the name of the elders, also speaks in our name, in the name of all men. He is asking the question which we *all* have to put to Him.

34

Ever since He trod this earth of ours, men have run to Him, and asked Him, *all* of them. Some of them have asked hypocritically, others mockingly and sceptically, others again angrily and passionately—but when they have put this question they have expressed the misery and longing of humanity, for it is a question full of hidden anxiety, full of a secret hope that it might indeed be *He*. 'Are You the Christ, are You the Saviour for Whom we have waited long, are You God's presence for which we have panted, are You God's sovereignty which has been so long promised to us?'

The answer of Jesus only helps those who have truly asked the question without any reservations. In the remarkable way in which Jesus gives His reply, He reveals a secret contradiction in the questioning of the world about God. Men are not unmoved, they are asking questions, they do seek God, they also come to Jesus with their questions. But behind all their questions there is a secret condition—namely, that the answer must be one which the questioner desires to receive. But the man who asks honestly will no longer make such conditions. That man surrenders himself wholly to Him whom he questions; he knows his ignorance; all he is asking is that God will teach him what he needs to know. We can understand God's answer only if we are willing to give ourselves away entirely. Thus, everyone who believes that he is really seeking God ought to ask himself whether he is really seeking with the desire to find, or whether his further search is not the expression of the fact that while he may, it is true, have already received an answer from God, he does not like it, and therefore, being disappointed in God, he decides to go on seeking. When this happens, is not his 'seeking' a sign of the fact that he will continually evade a real divine answer, and is in reality running away from it? When Caiaphas put this question in the name of the Jewish people, it may have been pronounced with indignation, perhaps even with a feeling of horror at the senselessness of the question itself. For is it not against all reason to ask this wretched, fettered prisoner, a helpless Man in their hands, Who has been exposed to the brutality of the temple police and the soldiers, whether He is the Almighty Power of God, the One Who is to bring in the Kingdom of God? Jesus gives a plain answer to this question. His answer says more than He has ever said before—because He knows it will cost Him His life. He speaks very clearly, making them responsible for their very question, turning their question into a sign of the truth of His reply: 'You say that I am.' That is—'Although your conception of the Christ, and of Me Who am now standing before you, are as wide apart as heaven and hell—since you still ask this question, you yourselves witness to the fact that I am He!'

'But from now on the Son of Man shall be seated at the right hand of the power of God.' This 'now' is the eternal miracle. With this one word 'now' Jesus rises above all that the questioners can see before them. From our earthly point of view, it separates two worlds: the battered criminal on the Cross, and the eternal, victorious Christ. In Time they are separated; in Eternity they are integrated. He does not say 'later on'; He says 'from now on'. Even while He is suffering and allowing Himself to be judged by men, Jesus is operating with the Power of God and, in the language of the Gospel of John, He is being 'glorified'. That is why in His reply He contrasts the earthly shame with the invisible glory and majesty. In so doing He makes it evident to his questioners what is the judgment that their obstinacy and wilful blindness will receive. And He also reveals to His Church, to those who follow in the way of His sufferings, the consolation which awaits them. He warns us not to judge from what our eyes tell us, as we all tend to do. He warns us to close our eyes, and only to listen to His words. Only in this listening shall we hear the real truth. Only as we listen to Him can we see God present in lowliness, and strong in weakness.

So we hear, so the world hears, these words of Jesus: 'You say that I am.' It is not an indefinite or colourless statement—it is very definite. At that time teachers used to speak to their pupils about it; the priests used to speak of it to the people; everyone knew it, and only dared to think of it with reverence and awe. If the long-desired Messiah comes, then all He needs to say about Himself is this, 'I am He'—and all the world will bow down before him! If this Messianic self-disclosure is to be received from the lips of this impotent prisoner then there is no third way possible: *either* they must believe in Him, *or* they must be caused to stumble. The sharp sound, made by the tearing of the high priest's garment, the excited movements and cries with which this answer is greeted, show that the sentence had already been pronounced. They have asked—but what they hear is not a prophetic proclamation, but blasphemy. Indeed, the God of our desires, of our reason, of our values, is truly blasphemed where the true God is at work and reveals Himself! Blessed are they who are not offended in Him!

The mystery of the Passion story extends down to the choice of actual words. Those who are here sitting in judgment on Jesus, and who condemn Him to death for blasphemy, and for the arrogance of claiming to be the Messiah, are using words which they should be using, which those who follow Him and humbly confess him should be using to confess Him as their Judge and their Lord. For the question, 'Are You the Christ? Are You the Son of God?', is followed by the answer: 'What further testimony do we need? We have heard it ourselves from His own lips.' What else could *we* say to justify our confession? On what else could we base the fact that we staked everything upon this suffering Man, and that we expect everything from Him? Why is it that all men's 'rational' excuses, and all their 'obvious', superficial judgments, cannot shake faith from its foundation? What can we say to the world? The Church and its theologians have often tried to collect all sorts of proofs. But in so doing they have only concealed the truth about this Man Jesus Christ, rather than revealed Him. For indeed this is His truth: that where no proof can be seen, and where we see nothing but suffering and shame, there the greatest work of divine power is being achieved.

Faith means believing in the word of Jesus like a man who shuts his eyes and simply listens and hears, and thus in a new way learns to *see*. 'He Himself has said it.' To the Old Man, that is, a reason for condemning Him; but to the New Man the same words become the foundation of faith in Jesus. Why do we lift up our hearts and voices by an open grave and sing Easter hymns? Why are we comforted by the knowledge that our sins have been forgiven? Why, in an era of so much suffering and evil, do we still affirm that God is love? Why do we pray 'Our Father'? Why do we not fear and tremble—not even for our faith? Because we are *certain* that neither death nor life can separate us from the love of God. Why? What are our guarantees? 'What further testimony do we need? We have heard it ourselves from His own lips.'

V

Luke 23.1-12

Then the whole company of them arose, and brought Him before Pilate. And they began to accuse Him, saying, 'We found this Man perverting our nation, and forbidding us to give tribute to Caesar, and saying that He Himself is Christ a King.' And Pilate asked Him, 'Are you the King of the Jews?' And He answered him, 'You have said so.' And Pilate said to the chief priests and the multitudes, 'I find no crime in this Man.' But they were urgent, saying. 'He stirs up the people, teaching throughout all Judaea, from Galilee even to this place.'

When Pilate heard this, he asked whether the man was a Galilean. And when he learned that He belonged to Herod's jurisdiction, he sent Him over to Herod, who was himself in Jerusalem at that time. When Herod saw Jesus, he was very glad, for he had long desired to see Him, because he had heard about Him, and he was hoping to see some sign done by Him. So he questioned Him at some length; but He made no answer. The chief priests and the scribes stood by, vehemently accusing Him. And Herod with his soldiers treated Him with contempt and mocked Him; then, arraying Him in gorgeous apparel, he sent Him back to Pilate. And Herod and Pilate became friends with each other that very day, for before this they had been at enmity with each other.

So Pilate enters the creed! He could never have dreamed that his name would be more deeply engraved upon the memory of mankind than the names of all the Roman Emperors, and of all other rulers of mankind. In every creed his name reminds us that the redemption of which the

39

Gospel speaks is something *real*, an *event*, which actually took place here, upon this earth. It reminds us that Jesus of Nazareth was no mythical personage, but a real man. 'True Man, born of the Virgin Mary' as our catechism says, who was crucified on a particular date, in a particular country, under the Governor, Pontius Pilate. It also reminds us that the representative of the law of the state, in virtue of his office, had to confirm the fact that this Man, Whom he handed over to be crucified, was guilty of no crime at all. Further, it reminds us that the crucifixion of Jesus Christ, the killing of God upon this earth, was not due only to the Jews. Here, pagans as well as Jews are equally involved. Here the hostility of all men towards God's Messenger is revealed.

How little does a man know of the significance of his actions! Pilate was evidently wholly unaware of the significance of the situation with which he had to deal; to him it was a small matter, and a very unpleasant one into the bargain. Yet the question at stake was really this, how the coming of God upon the earth would end, what kind of reception men would give Him. The fact that God's coming into the world ended in His death was not an accident. It was the necessary revelation of the truth that the whole of mankind is living in *sin*, which means in a state of strange and hostile alienation of all human life from its primal source, an alienation which involves every sphere of our life in a rebellion against God. It was for this that Jesus went to the Cross. As we read the Gospel story, we must all be struck by the fact that when Jesus passed by, on the way of the Cross, all the individual types of this alienation are brought out into the open. Jesus only needed to come near and the demons began to stir; they could no longer have it all their own way. If Jesus had *not* gone this way, then Peter and the rest of his friends would probably have been faithful, grateful and reliable followers. If Jesus had not got in the way of Annas and Caiaphas, they would probably have remained upright, worthy and astute high priests. If He had not met the Pharisees, they would probably have remained fanatical, it is true, but otherwise, at bottom, quite innocuous, bourgeois citizens. If He had not encountered Pilate, Pilate would probably have merely been one of the energetic, determined Roman officials who were so well able to combine their own interests with those of the state; and Herod would have been one of the many liberal and jovial princes and *littérateurs* of his own day.

A man's attitude towards Jesus *seems* to be 'only' a religious question. In reality, it is a question which affects his whole existence. The way in which a poet or a politician or a thinker regards Jesus *seems* to be important only from the religious point of view. Actually a man cannot be a serious poet, or a responsible politician, if he regards his attitude towards Jesus as a side-issue, or as something that can safely be ignored, for it is precisely at this point that his whole being, his real being comes out. The value of his work as a whole is revealed in this encounter. Thus the attitude of a Roman official towards Jesus Christ, in an apparently purely political matter, was not merely one element in his behaviour as a whole. For Caiaphas this single encounter decided the meaning of the conduct of the high priest; and for Pilate, it affected the basis and the value of all his work as a servant of the state. Here, by an infallible test, the fundamental basis of their behaviour, whether it was truth or deceit, was brought to light. Thus a man's attitude towards the Gospel reveals whether he is discharging his office and his mission—which he has received from God—for himself, or for God. Inner truth and inner deceit are brought to light when Jesus Christ passes by.

The Passion story shows us, first of all, in the light of this ruthless test, the inner collapse of the ecclesiastical order of Israel. Judas and Peter are shown to be, each in their own way, liars. But this is no less true of the chief priests and the scribes. They behave as though they were concerned solely with the glory of God, which must not be infringed. But what they really care about is their own reputation, the value of their piety, the authority of their decrees. The eagerness with which

41

they now accuse the rejected Messiah as an enemy of the state is deceitful. *Apparently* concerned for the good of the Roman state, they really hate it from the bottom of their hearts. *Seemingly* indignant about supposedly revolutionary activity, they are actually only too ready to support it at any time. This inner situation confuses them to such an extent that for the sake of their own self-preservation they are willing to throw over what, until then, had been their most sacred possession : their belief in the Messiah or the Messianic hope. For we must be quite clear about this : from their own point of view, a Messiah, when he comes, can do nothing other than urge people to refuse to pay taxes to Rome, and to fight against Roman rule. Hence in denouncing Jesus to the Roman Governor they were renouncing their Messianic hope altogether, and handing themselves over to Rome. They were rejecting the Messiah; they were giving to pagans the right to try the Messiah; and in so doing they were betraying the whole hope of their nation. This means that the whole meaning of Israel has been abandoned. To such lengths can deceit drive man! It is a significant and sinister fact that when a man bases his whole life upon this kind of untruth—when he is only pretending to be concerned with the glory of God, when all he really wants is to exercise his own love of power —in the end he cannot be faithful in anything else; he cannot keep his word; he seems to be compelled to be disloyal to all his former ideals; the further he goes along this path, the more inextricably he becomes entangled in the net he has woven; his whole life is in confusion. It was the most fateful hour in the history of the people of Israel when the chief priests and the elders said to the Roman Procurator, 'This Man is your enemy'. From that day forward, the Messiah was lost to the People of God; henceforth the Jew moves through history feeling homeless and 'lost', because his whole 'home' was in this belief in the Messiah as the Divine Deliverer. That is why a Jew can be saved from this desolation only by finding Jesus Christ, the Messiah of his people.

Now it was no accident that Jesus was condemned both by the ecclesiastical and the political authorities. It was not a couple of fanatics who had Him put to death. It was not due to an excited mob—nor even to a crowd which had been led astray by propaganda, like that which stoned His first martyr, Stephen, at the city gates. No, He was 'eliminated' by means of a formal trial, with a formal sentence, and a public execution. This means that the political accusation, brought by the chief priests, was a lie, but would not have been possible had there not been some occasion for it. This occasion consisted in the fact that although, certainly, the aim of Jesus was not political, the influence of His work profoundly affected the life of the state. No sphere of life can escape the consequences of His coming. Hence we cannot read and reflect upon this trial of Jesus before Pilate too seriously. For here human authority is confronted by the authority which has granted this power. Here God Himself is being accused by His servants. Thus God Himself has become a great open question for the Government.

The Bible avoids speaking of these questions in general terms such as 'Church and State', or 'Politics and Religion', or similar phrases. Rather it fixes the responsibility on the individual person; in his personal responsibility it speaks quite concretely of this or that particular person. For this particular man, for Pilate, there is no 'religious' question which is not at the same time a political question. He is now asked, in his official capacity, how he ought to discharge his office, that office which God has given him (for all authority is from God) —which does he want to serve? The fidelity or the self-seeking of his official behaviour must come out plainly. Whether the fear of God is there, is not only a religious question. It is —and we know this from our own army orders—a thoroughly military question; this comes out clearly in the encounter of the Procurator with Jesus. It will equally certainly become a political question. Here we see that the actual decisions of history are not taken in the light of the 'justice' or 'injustice'

43

of systems and programmes, but in the light of actual persons —their truth and their deceit. Carl Hilty has said somewhere, very truly: 'A man who holds high public office . . . who fears something more than God, is a miserable creature.' Pilate was a 'miserable creature' in this sense. Later, it is true, he was denounced to the Emperor Caligula for some particular cruelties, but it may be assumed that then his enemies were exaggerating matters. Pilate was not a particularly wicked man, not a criminal; he was only a man who did not fear God, but was full of other fears. He was afraid of the Jews, he was afraid of the mob, he feared the influential leaders of the Jewish people, he feared being denounced to the Emperor, perhaps he was even a little afraid of this Man Jesus Himself, this enigmatic Person Who was standing before him. He was harassed by fears of all kinds, hence this whole affair was so unpleasant for him; that is why he was so painfully surprised when the Jews turned the matter into a political question. That is why (as a man who is afraid always does) he tried to put the responsibility on to the shoulders of someone else, that is why he jumped at the word 'Galilee', and sent Jesus over to the ruler of Galilee, to Herod. And that is why, when no other way seemed possible, he perverted the law.

So, in His last hours, Jesus was surrounded by people who showed by their behaviour what is the real state of man, what that humanity, which He had come to save, is really like, fundamentally. This revelation becomes ever clearer and ever more terrible: first of all there is the fanaticism and the anger of the Jews, then the irresponsibility and timidity of the authorities who wield political power; and then finally, as a dreadful climax, the scene at Herod's palace, where Jesus Christ, the very presence of God upon earth, becomes the sport of Herod and his court. When the Bible wants to show the lost condition of man it does not describe criminals and convicts, but the appalling blindness and unawareness of average human beings, the blindness of the educated, of the bourgeois, of high officials, the blindness of us all, even of people like ourselves, who live in Lichterfelde and Dahlem.[1] Can we ever forget, can we ever cease to hear that scornful chatter, the cruel laughter of the courtiers and their ladies, who join in Herod's laughter: 'And Herod with his soldiers treated him with contempt and mocked him.' And was it not inevitable that at this point the two official rulers should come together? The brotherhood of Jesus Christ created fellowship in the Holy Catholic Church beyond all the divisions of the world; it has its counterpart in the brotherhood of those who are Christ's enemies, which also triumphs over all other causes of disunion: 'And Herod and Pilate became friends with each other that very day, for before this they had been at enmity with each other.'

In this section of the Gospel, in which so little is said of Jesus, and so much of the different people in the narrative—in which, indeed, Jesus Himself almost disappears behind these terrible revelations of human nature at its worst—we are impressed by the fact that here we are not listening to a tale of long ago and of its evil deeds. This story uncovers *our* life: Pilate with his injustice due to fear; Herod with his desire for sensation in religious matters and his cynical mockery over the humiliation of the Saviour; the Jews, who would rather betray that which was most sacred to them as a people than submit to God's revelation of Himself. All this is a possibility, no, a reality, of our own life, the reality which brought Jesus to the Cross. These people in the story, with their deceitfulness and deliberate wickedness, do not stand alone. In the sight of *God*, we too are involved in the same guilt. It is *we* who nail Jesus to the Cross, who say 'No' to God, who have our own fantasy idols and Messiahs, who brush aside God's commandments as too tiresome, and daily reject His claims.

But it is precisely *because* God claims man for Himself that Jesus allows Himself to be executed. He does not offer a passive sacrifice; He gives Himself up freely and deliberately.

[1] Suburbs of Berlin (*Translator*).

45

That is why the heart of this passage is the verse in which Pilate asks: 'Are you the King of the Jews?' He puts this question as a Roman. By it he means: 'Are you really the Messiah whom the Jews are expecting? Are you the One who will bring them salvation? or deliverance?' Jesus does not reply: 'I am,' because then Pilate would misunderstand this politically. Nor does he say: 'I am not' (that is, as the Jews mean it), for then Pilate would also misunderstand it. Jesus replies: 'You have said so.' By this He means: 'Your words are correct, although the meaning of My Kingship is quite different from anything that you or the Jews mean by it.' The meaning of the Kingdom of Jesus Christ is the freedom of man for God.

All the people involved in this story are men who are profoundly 'un-free'. Pilate has power, but not freedom. *You* are not free if you are 'enlightened', like Herod; you are not free if you have power like Pilate; you are not free, if you lie as easily as the elders. So it goes on—the possibilities are endless. You are not free, if you can bend the law to your own ends, if for you the end justifies the means, if you run with the hare and with the hounds, if through silence in the face of injustice, or through compromise in face of violence, or through submission to deceit you gain respect and honour and power for yourself. But you *are* free when the Son makes you free; you are free when you place yourself at the disposal of the will of God. In Jesus Christ the world is shown the one Man whose whole being is dedicated to the will of God. And Jesus Christ invites us to allow Him so to influence us, by His word, and His power, that all our bonds may be broken. That is why Jesus went to the Cross. In so doing He makes it clear that all our own efforts to achieve freedom only lead to this: that we put God, the fountain of life, to death, and take the guilt of His death upon our own shoulders. But at the same time He destroys the power of death; He builds a wall round all our fears; as we follow Him, when we allow ourselves to be led by Him, he makes us entirely free from all our fears;

46

He makes us impregnable in the midst of all dangers.

'The Lord is on my side; I will not fear what man doeth unto me' (Ps. 118.6). Thus Jesus sang with His disciples on the evening before His death. Already He was singing the song of resurrection before His death. This makes us certain that we, too, at the end of that road which we now tread with Him, will also sing Easter hymns. We can sing them even now. The praise that rises from the hearts of those who have entered into the glorious liberty of the children of God is the distinctive mark of the way of Christ and of His disciples.

Luke 23.13-25

Pilate then called together the chief priests and the rulers and the people, and said to them, 'You brought me this Man as one who was perverting the people; and after examining Him before you, behold, I did not find this Man guilty of any of your charges against Him; neither did Herod, for he sent Him back to us. Behold, nothing deserving of death has been done by Him; I will therefore chastise Him and release Him.'

But they all cried out together, 'Away with this Man, and release unto us Barabbas'—a man who had been thrown into prison for an insurrection started in the city, and for murder. Pilate addressed them once more, desiring to release Jesus; but they shouted out, 'Crucify, crucify Him!' A third time he said to them : 'Why, what evil has He done? I have found in Him no crime deserving death; I will therefore chastise Him and release Him.' But they were urgent, demanding with loud cries that He should be crucified. And their voices prevailed. So Pilate gave sentence that their demand should be granted. He released the man who had been thrown into prison for insurrection and murder, whom they asked for; but Jesus he delivered up to their will.

T H E Cross is the mirror of the world. In the Cross we see the real nature of the world, and where its way will end. It is not surprising that along the way of the Cross the different people who appear, one after the other, should have their real significance revealed. Pilate is the revelation of the person who thinks that the decision which confronts him in Jesus can be evaded, and who with his attempts at evasion becomes more and more entangled in his guilt, and is finally guilty of the death of God. There is nothing upon this earth which does not force us to decision through its relation to God. Each gift which each of us has been granted, however small and insignificant it may seem, is fully developed and fulfilled only when it is fulfilled in God, through the service in which we place it at God's disposal. But likewise, every fault which we have, however insignificant it may seem, may tomorrow be a blow in the face of the suffering Christ, may tomorrow lead you finally to find yourself shouting with the crowd: 'Crucify, crucify Him! Away with Him!' And every refusal of responsibility, however well justified it may be, and apparently reasonable, may today be the reason why, all of a sudden, you begin to behave like Pilate, who was unfaithful to his official duty, ran away from responsibility, and allowed Christ to be nailed to the cross. We are living in a time when far and wide among the nations this accusation is still being brought against Christ. Today, just as then, He, with His Church, is suspected of being a danger and a source of unrest. Therefore His Church must look with care into this mirror of the Passion story, and learn from it that it was not only the fanatical cold hatred of godlessness which led to the world saying 'No' to God. The narratives of the Evangelists are restrained, and, so far as may be, confined to facts. But here they show very plainly something which cannot be overlooked—that the guilt of Man for the death of the Divine Deliverer was due not only to this hatred, but just as much to thoughtlessness, lack of decision, self-concern, and unfaithfulness in official duty.

Thus in the Passion story Pilate represents those people who 'would like' to act rightly, but do not decide to do so. He 'would like' to save this Man Jesus. It cannot be denied that Pilate was on the side of Jesus. He went so far in his attempts to save Him that people may have begun to wonder why he took such an interest in the question of releasing Jesus. We do not know the reason for this concern. Perhaps it was caused

49

by his wife's dream, as recorded by another evangelist : 'Have nothing to do with that righteous Man, for I have suffered much over Him today in a dream' (Matt. 27.19). Perhaps there was a relic of superstition in his mind? Or perhaps it was the way Jesus looked at him which made Pilate feel uneasy? Possibly Pilate may even have been slightly influenced by this remarkable Man? In any case he *wanted* to set Him free, and he assured the Jews several times over that he found no reason to order His execution. But he—and possibly you see yourself reflected in him—is the type of man who would 'like' to do good, but only on condition that he need not take any risks, who thinks he wants to commit himself, but never really does so.

So it was inevitable that with all these half-hearted efforts to set this prisoner free, Pilate only became more deeply involved in this difficult situation. First of all he tried to relieve himself of responsibility by sending Jesus to Herod. Then he thought he would be very clever and get the Jews themselves to clamour for the release of Jesus, in order that they might assume the responsibility themselves, instead of leaving it to him. He tried to twist the matter round, in such a way that it would look as though he were only doing them a favour if he released Jesus—as if in so doing he were only carrying out *their* wishes. He hoped that the nation, which, he was well aware, was full of tension and distrust of the occupying Power, would regard this Man as their representative, and would choose Him as the prisoner who was usually released at their request at this festival. Thus it was inevitable that as Pilate struggled to evade his official responsibility he became more and more entangled and 'un-free'. For now he had tacitly put himself into the hands of the people, and in so doing had renounced the official duty with which he had been entrusted. He was at the mercy of the mood of the mob. By putting this question to the masses he played into their hands. He 'would like' to do the right thing, and release this innocent Man, but he did not 'will' it, actually, and under all circumstances;

hence from the outset he was a defeated man, whose actions contradicted his words: for instance, he wanted to release Jesus, but said that he would have Him scourged first. But why should an innocent man be scourged at all? And then he said that he would set Him free, but he spoke as if Jesus had already been sentenced, and thus could be released on this day, according to custom. How could he possibly put Jesus of Nazareth, in Whom he found 'no crime at all', upon the same level as the revolutionary and murderer, Barabbas? But when the mob began to shriek 'Crucify, crucify Him!' Pilate was caught, no choice was left to him. Again and again he tried to persuade the people to choose Jesus of Nazareth, but as they hurled their cries at him, already in his own mind he could hear accusations being laid against him by informers to the suspicious Emperor Tiberius. Indeed, he knew that the Emperor was under the influence of a favourite from whom no good could be expected. He was also aware that there were already a good many men in Rome who had no greater desire than to hold the office of Procurator in Palestine. He knew all this, and as he brooded over it he felt it was impossible to do what, in his heart of hearts, he *knew* to be his duty.

And then he began to wonder how far he ought to go in this situation. He wanted to give just judgment, it is true, but this innocent Man was not so important to him, after all; at least. He was not sufficiently important to make him renounce his official position, his independence and his authority. So Pilate took the line of a judge who puts something else in the place of the divine law which he has been appointed to administer upon this earth. Above and beyond this divine law he took other considerations into account; he was open to a good many other suggestions. So Pilate the judge became a murderer, and the hour when justice upon earth was at stake became an opportunity for a crafty alliance.

On this day, therefore, all the people involved in this situation were united against Christ—even all those who had hitherto been divided. Up to that moment Herod and Pilate had been bitter enemies. For Pilate, Herod had been only one of those tiresome kinglets of Syria. For Herod, Pilate had been the man who reduced his own authority, because he was the official placed over him by Rome. On this day these two men did not merely exchange formal courtesies, but, in a surprising way, they became friendly. In the story of the trial of Jesus we see people who are usually despised by the chief priests, and who are themselves very distrustful of them, becoming one with the ruling class; similarly, the Jewish leaders—who are otherwise full of fierce hatred for the Roman rule—on this day seem to be concerned *for* it. Thus everybody seems to be united at one point! For the things that divide them from one another are all much less important than the one thing which divides them from this Man who is standing before them. All the other causes of division are merely human; but that which divides them from this Man is the deep gulf between God and Man, between the Holy One and the rebel. That is why they are united. It was a unity in 'un-freedom'.

There is nothing fortuitous in the Passion Story. Pilate, who was now so anxious to avoid being denounced to the Emperor, and for this reason was willing to sacrifice this Man Jesus, was, as we know, later on a victim of the very charge he was now trying to avoid. Finally he was denounced and accused to the Emperor; then all he could do was to open his veins in the bath, in order to escape being sentenced to death. In that last hour, as he saw the water turning red with his own blood, did he, we wonder, look back to that day when he had previously tried to avoid being denounced? Perhaps he then realised that it is impossible to run away—that if you run away with the aid of injustice, the danger is still there, and what you have put aside with the aid of unjust means will one day come back with still greater force. Perhaps it will come back in a different form, but still it will be true that this time there will be no hope, there will be no way out; the full force of the disaster will overwhelm you.

On the other hand, it is also true that there is nothing accidental in the fact that this man Pilate who tried to avoid making a great decision, and tried to throw it upon the Jewish people, still became God's instrument; that is, through his action, God gave the Jews once more, finally, the power to make the right decision. So, too, it is not accidental that—as is recorded in some ancient manuscripts—the revolutionary Barabbas, who was here set up against Jesus of Nazareth, was also called 'Jesus'. This was the question Israel had to decide. They had to decide between two men called 'Jesus'—*Jesus Barabbas*, or *Jesus of Nazareth*. Which one did they want?

That is the eternal theme of the decision which confronts us, both Church and nation. The name 'Jesus' means 'God saves' (or 'helps'). Whence, O Man, do you look for God's help? How will it come? Through a change in external conditions, which was the aim of Barabbas? Or through a complete change in your own heart? Will it come through the struggle to assert your own will, at all costs? Or through the struggle to make God's will prevail for the Kingdom of God? Through an outward or an inward conflict? Through the conflict which begins with repentance, with the sense of guilt, and with self-renunciation? Israel was a very religious nation. The strict legal piety of the Pharisees has probably never been exceeded by any other body of men, down to the present day, and it was a high-watermark of human piety. Thus it is evident that we can have God's law in our heads and in our wills, and take the name of God upon our lips quite seriously; we can have very high ideals; we do not need to be in any way sub-human, godless, or materialistic; indeed, we may be idealistic champions of all that is right and good—and still we may murder the 'Help of God', the Saviour; we may say 'No' to the coming of God, and be on the side of Antichrist.

It is no accident that one of the last human scenes which Jesus saw was the scene of the shouting crowd. Perhaps many people shouted with the others, although they had no idea what it was all about, and they only took part in the noise because others were doing it. That is mass action, which means that no one in particular feels responsible, at least scarcely anyone : everyone can shout and everybody repeats what the others say, and then hides behind them. The Bible, however, certainly does not make excuses for man simply because he belongs to the masses. It addresses each individual person in this mass, and asks him : 'How did you come to behave like this? Do you know what you are saying when you shout like this? *You* are guilty!' And the very fact that the Bible speaks thus to the individual makes the individual (in accordance with God's purpose in creating him) a *man*, who must act on his own responsibility, who has his own conscience, and is particularly and personally addressed by God—just as each individual alone, and by himself, has to die his own death. Because nothing in the Passion story is accidental, the most varied forms of human decision—from the most fully conscious and deliberate to the dim, sub-conscious decision of the masses—are all saddled with responsibility. All are marked with the one word, *guilt*.

In this passage Jesus Himself does not utter a word. He seems to be merely an object, something about which people are arguing, exposed to being pushed about, and subject to their will. But is there anything more disquieting than such a passage in the Gospel, in which Jesus does not say a word? Can there be anything more disquieting than this silence of Jesus in the midst of all this tumult? In this silence is He not only *apparently* an object? Is He not actually wholly the Subject, the one free *Person*, among people who are all unfree? It is He who sets all this excitement in motion. It is His glance that forces Pilate again and again to make a feeble effort for justice. It is His very existence that forces the high priest to feel that he cannot be content merely to see Jesus arrested and beaten and impotent. They only need to look at Him as He stands there, without moving, and looks at them, to know that they can never get rid of Him except by having Him put to death. The disquieting silence of Jesus is the hidden action of Jesus in this story.

In a striking passage in the Book of Acts (4.23-31), there are some strange words. The Church in Jerusalem is singing and praying in the spirit of the second psalm, which speaks of kings and rulers, arrayed against the Lord, and against His Anointed. And then they go on in their prayer to say: 'Truly in this city there were gathered together against Thy Holy Servant Jesus, whom Thou didst anoint, both Herod and Pontius Pilate, with the Gentiles and the peoples of Israel, *to do whatever Thy hand and Thy plan had predestined to take place.*'

What does this mean? Surely it means this. Pilate and the Jews, the people and the high priest, were wholly guilty, fully responsible for their decision. But in this decision they could not move a finger without doing what had been purposed by the counsel of God. They think that *they* are acting, and that they are getting rid of God, and yet, in spite of their guilt, all they are doing is to help to bring God's cause to a victorious conclusion, as God had determined. From that day, this is the truth which the Christian Church has always perceived when Christ is being attacked. The one who attacks Him is guilty, it is true, but by his action he simply reveals man's enmity to the will of God; in this 'No' we see the wickedness and deceit of the human heart. On the other hand, he who attacks Christ does nothing that cannot be used by God for the good of the Church, and the salvation of the world. The Church sees this foreshadowed in a remarkable way in the Old Testament. There Joseph says to his brothers, when he makes himself known to them in Egypt: 'Do not be distressed, or angry with yourselves, because you sold me here: for God sent me before you to preserve life. . . . So it was not you that sent me here, but God' (Gen. 45.5-8). When Christ is put to death, He becomes the sign of hope for the world which killed Him. Thus everyone who is arrested for Christ's sake, every martyr, every day of suffering for Christ is honoured by God. Then it becomes an honour to suffer; it becomes a gift—what a paradox, that it should be a gift! It becomes a sign of hope for a time which—without this suffering—would seem more hopeless than any other. The end of the ways of God is glory. When the Church proclaims this truth, it is based on the great experience which she met at the Cross of Christ, and which has been confirmed again and again all down the centuries of her history.

At the present time no one can help feeling deep misgiving and concern for the destiny of Man. Indeed no one can love his country, and not share in deep concern for its need.[1] A man who loves his country sees things as they really are; but someone who only loves himself closes his eyes and gives himself up to illusory dreams. But in all our cares and anxieties to-day we are moving towards the festival of Easter. Then we shall be singing Easter hymns. *Lebendig Christus kommt herfür* ('The Living Christ comes forth') we shall sing with joy. As we tread this path, we realise that the fellowship of suffering of the Church with the Living Christ is not a sign of desolation but a sign that 'the Lord will never forsake His people'. Thus the silent Christ has the whole power of victory. In the silent fellowship of the witnesses to Christ there lies a great strength and a sign of hope. Sometimes we say, rather carelessly, that the Protestant Church is in a period of serious decline. That is an ungrateful saying. It seems to me that the Church of an earlier day was far more 'run-down' and disintegrated than that which is now working and preaching and witnessing to our nation. We have all had great experiences; in these years our eyes have been opened to things eternal— to the things which are essential for the life of our nation. For this we should be very grateful. The fact that this is happening amongst us is a sign that God has not forsaken us, that He still has some great purpose for us.[2] None of us should allow ourselves to lose the certainty that the Easter victory

[1] This sermon was preached at the height of Hitler's 'New Order' (*Translator*).
[2] Thanksgiving for the courage of the German 'Confessing Church' is implied here (*Translator*).

of Christ is the present strength of His Church. So let us all join in thanking Him upon our knees, that God has given us such signs of His presence and His mercy. So we shall be better prepared in the future to be better witnesses to Jesus Christ. With the help of God's Word we shall be better prepared to fight against the Pilate in our own hearts, and not to betray the freedom of the children of God.

VII

Luke 23.26-31

And as they led Him away, they seized one Simon of Cyrene, who was coming in from the country, and laid on him the cross, to carry it behind Jesus. And there followed Him a great multitude of the people, and of women who bewailed and lamented Him. But Jesus turning to them said, 'Daughters of Jerusalem, do not weep for Me, but weep for yourselves, and for your children. For, behold, the days are coming when they will say, "Blessed are the barren, and the wombs that never bore, and the breasts that never gave suck!" Then they will begin to say to the mountains, "Fall on us"; and to the hills, "Cover us." For if they do this when the wood is green, what will happen when it is dry?'

HE has done good to all. He has helped us all, but no one helps Him. Now He is carrying His Cross and going forward, quite alone. The way of the Cross shows us the great loneliness of Jesus Christ. The cross-beam which will be nailed to the upright beam on Golgotha is now rubbing His back, which is still bleeding from the scourging. He is the image of a humanity which has been exposed to all weathers. Since the Last Supper, not a bite has passed His lips. From one court to another He has been dragged about, sleepless, beaten, insulted, spit upon, and He makes no resistance. He does not ask for anything; he does not ask that this cup may pass Him by, He is quite prepared to drink it to the last dregs. So He goes on His way, and we who have every reason to thank Him—we for whose sakes He came and dwelt among us—we who have received nothing but good from Him—we have forsaken Him.

That is the very essence of sin, and of the sins which we have come here today to confess. All these particular sins of omission and commission are *sin*, in the fact that we have separated ourselves from God, at the very moment when we should have clung to Him. We, His disciples, who have professed to be willing to go to death for Him, and are grateful to Him—*we* have done this. This is the real heart of sin : that we have forsaken God in His wrestling for the soul of the world. We have left Him all alone as He gives Himself up for us in order to save this world, His world, our world.

Every time that you have followed your own desires instead of the way of obedience to His will, every time that you have listened to the voice of your own wishes, and not to those which He has expressed, every time that you have avoided the shame of confessing His name before men, and have chosen a life without such conflicts, every time that you have allowed a poor brother of Jesus Christ to suffer and to carry his cross alone, and have not rushed to help him, every time that you have closed your heart to the suffering and needs of others, because you were selfish, or because you were preoccupied, or too lazy or too cold-hearted, or too pharisaical—on all these occasions you have left Him alone on His way to the Cross, and you have joined the crowd which simply 'looked on' as He went forward—to the Cross.

The section of humanity represented by the Roman soldiers was much too tough and hardened to be able to feel anything at all. A soldier who had been all over the world would have seen too many horrors, and taken part in too many terrible things, and indeed would have been forced to do so, to have any thought to spare for the poor criminal who was being led away to execution. But humanity is also represented by the Jewish women, who, as the custom was, accompanied the poor criminal with loud cries of lamentation on the way to execution. It was certainly a good custom, and it reveals more

59

humanity than is often shown nowadays in similar circumstances. But still—it was only a custom. Probably the lamentations did not come from a real, sudden, terrified awareness,
springing from the heart. After all, it *was* only a custom—a
lamentation which did not come from the heart. Beneath the
superficial emotions, these women were not deeply moved.

Finally, humanity is represented by this man, Simon of
Cyrene, this peasant, probably a man who had returned from
Africa (that is why Cyrene comes into the picture), who is
coming back from the fields. He wants to get home. He is
tired. On no account does he want to be mixed up in this
affair. He may have heard a good deal about this Man; he may
indeed have some cause to be grateful to Him, perhaps at one
time he cherished some hopes concerning Him—but now he
thinks to himself, 'Anyone can see there was nothing in it!
For Jesus has alienated both His own people, and the foreign
rulers as well! It will be best to keep out of this altogether,
and have nothing to do with Him!' It was only the blows of
the Roman soldiers which forced him to carry that Cross,
which they were too proud to touch. He did it very unwill-
ingly, resisting as long as he could, only giving in when forced
to do so, possibly even gnashing his teeth as he did so. For
who would want to carry the cross of a criminal?

So the only human help which Jesus Christ received on His
last earthly journey was not given for His own sake. He only
had the unwilling assistance of a man who was forced to help
a condemned criminal. But if He trod this way alone, it was
in order that you should never have to tread your way alone.
He was forsaken, and even forsaken by you, in order that *you*
might never be forsaken. What makes us feel more 'alone'
than our own special cross? What makes it more difficult to
bear than the fact that each of us has to bear it *alone*? And
Jesus trod this way to the very end, in order that *you* need not
taste the final depths of this loneliness. So He did not let Himself be 'put off' by your sinful lack of faith, but He went on
His way to the end, in order that *you* might have the great

comfort and help and strength which upheld Him in His last hours. That is the way He trod to the end; there was no hope of rescue, there was only death. Henceforth there is no cross without Christ, no crime without mercy, no shame without the glory of God.

Simon resisted the shame until he was forced to accept it. Yet in spite of his resistance, to the Church he has become a symbol of her own pilgrimage. So the Church goes on her way alone, just as Simon, without knowing it, followed the way. In an ancient manuscript we read: 'They . . . laid on him the cross, *to carry it behind Jesus.*' 'Behind Jesus', and nowhere else; and we know quite well what that means. The Word of God tells us that this is not a simple matter. In practice this way of shame, when it is presented to us, cuts right across all our own desires. And when Jesus tells a disciple that he can only be a disciple if he takes up his cross and follows him, then he does not think only of the suffering, but of the shame. The Cross is the sign of shame, of being despised and rejected (Mark 15.28; Isa. 53.12). 'Where I am there shall my servant be also' (John 12.26). Yes, we shall be above, in glory—but only when we have trodden the *Via Dolorosa*, the way of the Cross and shame.

That is the revolution of values at which the world shudders. And which of us does not belong to the world at this point? However, the new values are full of the Gospel, and of hope. Nowhere else has it ever been discovered that suffering is a gift of God, that suffering is the veil which conceals blessing. Nowhere else do we see man dying not only with stern composure and heroism, but with *gladness*. The natural man— Simon of Cyrene—resists this with all his might. The New Man *desires* what the Old Man resists. And to our world it seems so senseless to do what the New Man tries to do—to welcome what the Old Man meets with a curse. The New Man says, like his Lord: 'Yea, Father, from my very heart I say, lay on me what Thou wilt! I will bear it.'

The Gospel of Mark suggests (15.23) that in his own family

61

Simon of Cyrene saw the confrontation of the Old and the New Man. He saw the Old Man later on, when he looked back and thought of the way he had fought against being forced to carry the Cross. He saw the New Man when he looked at his own sons. It seems that these sons, Alexander and Rufus, belonged to the church at Rome. At the end of the Epistle to the Romans (16.13) there comes a greeting: 'Greet Rufus, eminent in the Lord.' Possibly this Rufus is the son of Simon. It is indeed possible that this very Rufus, with the rest of the church in Rome, had to tread the way of the Cross under Nero—but not with resistance like his father's in those early days, but joyfully. The Roman writers of those days describe for us, with unconcealed amazement, how those Christians died.

Simon carried the Cross 'behind Jesus'—and in so doing he has become the lasting image of the way of the Church. She does not go ahead of Jesus. She does not carry the Cross ahead of Him. She does not push herself forward to do it. It is laid upon her, and then she carries it behind Jesus. And when she looks ahead, she does not see death, suffering, and the grave; she only sees *Christ* going ahead, before her. *Christo duce nihil triste* is an ancient Latin saying, which means: 'Nothing is sad when we are under the guidance of Christ.' The meaning of the Cross is transformed, and when we see it in every act of worship made over us as a sign of blessing, when we give it to the newly confirmed, when it is signed on our babies at their baptism and over communicants at the Lord's Supper— then something takes place, in order that we may be glad over the greatest transformation which is ever experienced upon earth.

When we read this passage to the end we understand that even the following scene, with the terrible words to the weeping women of Jerusalem, is included in the whole power of this Gospel. For it shows that this Man, dragging Himself so painfully along the way to death, a Man to whom every moment seems an eternity, is not simply 'enduring' all this in a dull, stupefied way, but that all His thoughts are not for Himself, but for others. These loud lamentations do not irritate or anger Him. He knows how much they are worth. In the midst of His own suffering He is grieved for these women, who do not know what terrible things they will one day have to endure. 'Jesus, turning to them, said, . . .' we read. These last words to His own people show what He felt about Israel : how He longed to take them 'under His wings', to win them for God, and for righteousness; how He grieved for the Church of God which refused to follow Him. At the same time they show how bitterly He realised that now nothing He could say, not even this last call to repentance, would have any effect, but that now, inevitably, judgment would fall upon them. Perhaps one or two of these women did at least understand this : that the judgment He was foretelling would be a time of sheer despair. For that is what it means to say that those who are 'unfruitful' will be 'blessed'. To a Jewish woman 'unfruitfulness' was her greatest sorrow, and to bear children her greatest joy. This was due to the fact that every man child who was born might perhaps—who could tell?—be the Messiah. So a time in which unfruitfulness would be regarded as a blessing must be a time of hopeless judgment. Jesus knew why He proclaimed this now. The judgment fell upon the nation in a terrible form, a few decades later.

The mystery of these words of Jesus lies in the fact that in spite of this, in spite of all that He knows and sees, which they were unable to hear or to understand, He still went on His way. Although He saw the approaching judgment so clearly, He still went on the way of reconciliation. He was still saying to them : 'Do you not see in Me what lies before you—the severity and the seriousness of the love of God? See it now in Me!' When Jesus speaks of the 'green wood' he means something like this. If even the green, damp wood is burnt up in the devouring fire of God's judgment, what will happen to you, the 'dry wood', which lies there defenceless and useless, ready for burning, when God comes in judgment as the prophet foretold : 'For, behold, the Day comes, burning like an oven' (Mal. 4.1)

So Jesus speaks to His People—for the last time—and then goes on His way. And because He went on His way, we are able to come here today, we who are like 'dry wood', which at the coming of God will flare up and be destroyed. We who are nothing in ourselves, who cannot shield ourselves from, or avoid, this wrath; we come here to be protected. This indeed is what happens to us at the Lord's Table. He who is ever-living, eternal, comes into our hearts, and enfolds us in His protecting and keeping power! He whom *we* have forsaken, will never leave us nor forsake us! Here and now, He confirms this once again.

So we come here to be strengthened and made firm in this faith; and then we know that this transformation will take place in us, the reversal of the pain and shame into the glory of the Cross. We are all sent forth to witness to this. For everyone who takes Christ seriously has to carry his share of the Cross and of its shame. But for everyone who awaits his cross, there also awaits the experience of being saved, and kept, and blessed, and glorified, so that in the end he can say : 'O sweet Cross! O good Way!' For the end is not death, but, thanks to the death of Christ, salvation, the entrance into the eternal kingdom of glory.

VIII

Luke 23.33-34

And when they came to the place which is called The Skull, there they crucified Him, and the criminals, one on the right and one on the left. And Jesus said, 'Father, forgive them, for they know not what they do.' And they cast lots to divide His garments.

So that is our God! As the proclamation of a prince or a magistrate is nailed to a board, in order to proclaim the will of the authorities, so is He nailed to a tree. That is the way in which God makes Himself known to us. If we dare believe the evidence of our eyes, can we see anything other than the most wretched picture of humanity possible to conceive—the figure of One exposed to every kind of torture? Anyone who demands to see signs of God's power cannot help being offended at the sight. Anyone who takes as his standard his own intellect, his human wisdom, and his own conception of what he is prepared to believe about God,—what can he do other than exclaim: 'Folly and senselessness!' And so the Jews, and people like them, have always been exasperated by this sight, and have talked indignantly of a 'scandal'; and the Greeks, and people like them, have mocked at its 'senseless folly'; while we—that is why we are here together today—we see our God nailed to a tree (I Cor. 1.22-24).

This is no easy matter. It is good to face it squarely. Here we see God manifesting Himself; and since He first hung here, the soldiers who did the deed have been joined by countless others, who have wanted to achieve the same end. Here man has laid hands on God; men have exercised authority over Him. And He has allowed Himself to be nailed thus, in order to make Himself known—although *they* nailed Him to the Cross in order to make Him harmless, in order that He should be put out of action. And countless people have joined them in this attempt: princes and popes, ecclesiastics and statesmen, professors and politicians. Their actions and their words are aimed at nothing less than driving nails into the members of Christ in order to make Him impotent. And each of us may well ask ourselves whether in our own lives we have acted like this in order to make Christ impotent. God is indeed there; He has come into our life without asking us. He wills to be our Lord and Master, and the aim of the Crucifixion is precisely this, to make this Lordship ineffective. That is the reason why they nailed Him so firmly to the Cross. This shows how much room the world has for God, when He comes to it. What a little space! 'The earth is the Lord's, and all that therein is; the compass of the world, and they that dwell therein' (Ps. 24.1). So this is the space the earth has for its Lord: this narrow beam of wood standing between heaven and earth, that is the great throne, that is the Throne of David which had been foretold, the Throne of Glory which will endure for ever, the Throne of Grace, more glorious than all the others. The earlier one, we are told (I Kings 10.18ff), was a great throne of ivory, overlaid with the finest gold; there were six steps to the throne, and the top of the throne was round behind; there were arms on either side of the seat, and two lions standing, one at each side of the throne; and on the six steps there stood twelve lions. That was the throne in the palace of Solomon. And now we behold the better throne: a beam of wood, upon which the King is nailed and is being tortured to death. And *this* is happening to *God*.

In the days to come one of you who are here today may find himself exposed to the utmost brutality, handed over, helpless and defenceless, to the will and cruelty of men.[1] If that comes, think of this figure of the promised King, Who hangs there between heaven and earth. God has penetrated so deeply into our human life that He has not been afraid of the consequences, but having decided to come down to our level He chose the way of humiliation. What is all the humiliation of this world compared with this humiliation of God? What does it mean for anyone to be dishonoured, mocked, tortured —compared with this descent of God into the lowest depths? Now we see where this humiliation was bound to end. Now we see where the joy of Christmas has led. 'Our Brother was the Eternal Good'—and it is because of this that He is hanging there. So if ever any of us is nailed so fast that we cannot move hand or foot; if ever we are exposed to the heat of the sun and the anguish of burning thirst, without any relief; if ever our only companions at the end are criminals and out-casts, *then* we should remind ourselves that it was the body of Almighty God which hung upon the Cross; that the hands which were pierced were the hands of God; that the feet which were nailed to the Cross were those of the Messenger of God, who came in such beauty and love to proclaim peace upon earth.

And all this took place *for our salvation*. That is why St Luke sums up the true meaning of the whole of world history in this one brief sentence: 'There they crucified Him.' God beholds His earth and the nations; they have done some great and amazing things. It would be quite contrary to the truth to say that men have never done anything much, that they have not had great thoughts and ideals; they have learnt much, and have created great forms of life and of art, great forms of community and of power; great thoughts and high ideals have been eagerly sought. But when they came face to face with *God*, in spite of all this, all that happened was this:

[1] The preacher's predecessor, Dr Niemöller, was then in a concentration camp, and the preacher and several members of the congregation were under warnings (*Translator*).

'And they crucified Him.' So this is the meaning of the proclamation of the God nailed to the Cross: when Man and God
meet, one or the other has to die. That is why men put God
to death, that is why Jesus sees the menacing cloud of final
death looming over mankind. And that is why this final conversation of the Father with the Son, so far as men are concerned, opens up another possibility. For this is the wonder of
this last Word—that when God and Man meet, when you and
your God confront one another, something quite different
from rebellion against Him takes place, something outside
His judgment upon you, something quite different: *forgiveness*. Forgiveness is the theme of the last conversation between
the Father and the Son, so far as we men are concerned. But
this well-known Word from the Cross is very mysterious.

It is evident that while men are putting Jesus to death He
sees a great danger hanging over the men who are doing it.
This danger is the wrath of God. What does this mean? It
does not mean anything in the nature of revenge, but the
danger consists in the fact that God might make these men
who meet Him in such a way responsible for the decision
which they have made against Him, that *their* last word might
also be *His* last word. So 'forgive them' means simply: 'Father,
do not let the matter rest there! Let this decision which Man
has made against his own life not be the last thing that has
happened in the life of humanity!' 'Turn it away'—or as it
really means in the Greek, 'Let it go!'

Thus forgiveness always consists in the fact that you do not
pin down the person who has injured you to what he has
done; you do not keep him bound to his act. Any one of us
who is here and knows true repentance, bitter sorrow over his
own actions, knows that so long as our acts are not forgiven
they are like a prison in which we are confined, from which
we cannot escape. And it is for the other person to decide
whether he will let us out, whether he will release us from
the prison of our actions, or whether he will shut the door
upon us by refusing his forgiveness. So Jesus asks the Father

to 'set them free' from their decision, from their action.

This Word is so mysterious because Jesus adds the words: 'For they know not what they do.' Now it is plain that when He asks for forgiveness, it is because *guilt* is present, because no other entry is possible into the new life, save forgiveness. But why does He say: 'They do not know what they do'? For whom is He actually praying in these words? Only for the soldiers? Only for those who are ignorant? Does He make a distinction between those who do it quite deliberately, with their eyes open, and those who do it simply out of folly? Does He exclude the former from forgiveness, and only include the latter? Dare we hope only if we can say: 'We did not know what we were doing'? No, it is not so. When Jesus prays for the soldiers to be forgiven—and certainly they are the first who are concerned in this request—He is really saying that what they are doing incurs real guilt. Why do they do it, then? Is it not a matter of discipline? They cannot have long to reflect. Should they make a decision of their own whether here and now this particular Man ought to be executed or not? Is it not simply their military duty to do what they are doing? Is not that sufficient excuse? But Jesus says that for this very reason they are guilty. Because of military discipline, because of the thoughtlessness that is bound up with it, many a man has put God to death and crucified Christ. You must realise this: all this is no excuse!

In these last considerations we have really been thinking about Pilate. Probably he too did not 'know' what he was doing when he failed to do his duty. He wanted to execute justice, but, somehow, he did not quite manage it. But this is no excuse; he was guilty. And where we are concerned, how often do we sin in the same way—by indecision, failure in official duty, and allowing personal considerations to sway our judgment! To do this is to put God to death, to crucify Christ afresh. It is the same with the chief priests, the Pharisees, and the scribes. In every kind of sin there is a large element of obscurity; we do not 'see through' the temptation.

That is why, in our folly, we always try to make excuses for ourselves, we always think we can appeal to 'extenuating circumstances'. So when Jesus prays 'Father, forgive them', it shows very clearly that here He is dealing with *sin*—for our indecision, our thoughtless obedience to cruel orders, and, indeed, our ignorance itself, are sin.[2]

Everyone who, in his ignorance, puts God to death, because he does not know what he is doing (and he *could* know it) is guilty. He does not know because he does not want to know. Indeed he does not want to think about it, for what would be the result if he did? Ignorance is sin; that is the first point. Only in the spirit of forgiveness does the Son say to the Father : 'Lord, do not look at their guilt; see how confused they are and how they have been led astray. Do not look at the secret deep decision against Thyself, but look at all that has made the decision easy for them. Because Thou art willing to forgive, behold them as they are! Treat them as sick people, although actually they are guilty, and their ignorance is wilful.' If we want to understand the secret of this Word of Jesus, we must think of ourselves. We must think how *we* pray when we see someone we love becoming more and more fatally entangled in a net of his own making, becoming more and more frustrated and desperate, until he cannot be reached by any one, however strong and wise they are—he will not listen. How we long to seize this person, and get down to the roots of his being, in order that he may be set free. But we cannot. In this saying of Jesus which refers to Pilate, the soldiers, and the chief priests, and then to all of us, all who murdered Christ, we see that in His love He is penetrating to the roots of our being and is then holding us up to God. And the mystery of His prayer is this—He uses our very guilt as an argument for forgiveness. Men put Him to death, and that is their guilt; they 'do not know' whom they are putting to death, but it is a wilful ignorance. And He offers this to God as the reason for His suffering. In some manuscripts of the

A reference to the Nazis' underlings is implied here (*Translator*).

Gospel of Luke this prayer is not included in the text. Some commentators think that the verse was not originally in the Lucan narrative, but that only later, in the light of the Sermon on the Mount, was it interpolated. But it is more likely that the reverse is the case. Probably some of the scribes could not bear to think that the love and forgiveness of Jesus were turned towards those who had rejected Him—the Jews who persecuted Him, the Romans who sentenced Him to death, the brutal soldiers who nailed Him to the Cross.

But this is precisely the Gospel which the Church has to proclaim to the world. Here He embraces the whole world with His gaze, lifts it out of its guilt, and holds it up as a poor, sick, weak world before the Father. While they have taken His very clothes away from him, and are without any feeling for the thirst which He endures under the burning sun, while they sit beneath the Cross and throw dice for His clothes, while they have robbed Him of everything, and have reduced Him to the extreme of poverty—they and we all live upon the fact that for us He became so poor and weak and dying. For this we thank Him every day of our lives.

IX

Luke 23.35-43

And the people stood by, watching; but the rulers scoffed at Him, saying, 'He saved others; let Him save Himself, if He is the Christ of God, His Chosen One!' The soldiers also mocked Him, coming up and offering Him vinegar, and saying, 'If You are the King of the Jews, save yourself!' There was also an inscription over Him, 'This is the King of the Jews.'

One of the criminals who were hanged railed at Him, saying, 'Are You not the Christ? Save Yourself and us!' But the other rebuked him, saying, 'Do you not fear God, since you are under the same sentence of condemnation? And we indeed justly; for we are receiving the due reward of our deeds; but this Man has done nothing wrong.' And he said, 'Jesus, remember me when you come in Your kingly power.' And He said to him. 'Truly, I say unto you, to-day you will be with Me in Paradise'.

'THE people stood by, watching.' Ever since that day the whole of mankind has 'stood by, watching' this unforgettable execution. Some are mocking, indifferent, or contemptuous. Others are more sympathetic, but all they do is to shrug their shoulders, and perhaps feel slightly disturbed about what is said to have happened there. And you who are here today have come out from among these people, you have come forward, and you want to kneel at the Cross. Do you really know to Whom you are coming? For Him Who hangs there, it is very important that you should always know to Whom you

72

are coming, and that you should not lose sight of it. That is why at the Lord's Table He always reminds you of that hour when He spoke of pouring out His blood, and of the breaking of His body. He is reminding you of that hour when He was nothing but a Saviour who was mocked and derided. This is your God, to whom you are coming, and you must never forget this: a Saviour who is mocked and derided. There He hangs in utter loneliness—and if the solitude of His suffering can be intensified, it is by this mockery. It has come to this, that He is surrounded only by curious spectators. All who are most closely involved in this scene have no compassion at all, but are full of mockery and hatred. This is our God, a God at whom people laugh.

And you who have come here to confess your sins and to receive Communion, you must see the Gospel which is contained in this part of the Passion story. He who hangs here has indeed, of His own accord, exposed Himself to the fact that He is on the Cross. He has indeed given Himself, of His own accord, to this miserable situation. The Almighty Christ willed it so that He would be mocked. Part of the work of redemption is taking place here. The evangelists have no desire to spare us at this point. Again and again they underline the fact: He is a Saviour at whom people laugh. They emphasise this, because it is the Gospel. Before the interrogation He was mocked by the soldiers and they played the fool with Him; the elders and the chief priests made a spectacle of Him, and Herod and his whole court made merry over Him. And now at the very end this laughter and mockery reappear, as people mock at someone who has taken too much upon himself, or someone whose words are in blatant contradiction to his actual situation which everyone can see.

It is our redemption that is here at stake. The point is this: that here everything is frustrated which gave us any possibility of depending upon ourselves, of going our own way further, and making our protest to God. God does not defeat us by punishing us with fire and sword, but by going to work

73

in a totally different way from ours. He frustrates us by giving Himself wholly into our hands, by permitting us, with all our wisdom and reason, to do anything we like with Him—He allows us to vent all our rebelliousness upon Him, in the name of our imagined power and wisdom. The fact that He thus gives Himself into our hands—and that is the meaning of the Crucifixion as a whole—shows where our human 'wisdom', the wisdom which does not begin with the fear of the Lord, can lead: to the point where it laughs at God, where all it can see of God is God's weakness and foolishness, where its sight becomes so perverted, so twisted away from all that God really is, that it has no conception at all of the real situation, and so can only laugh in His face.

    ' "I will destroy the wisdom of the wise,
       And the cleverness of the clever I will thwart."
Where is the wise man? Where is the scribe? Where is the debater of this age? Has not God made foolish the wisdom of the world? For since, in the wisdom of God, the world did not know God through wisdom, it pleased God through the folly of what we preach to save those who believe. . . . For the foolishness of God is wiser than men, and the weakness of God is stronger than men. . . . God chose what is foolish in the world to shame the wise. . . .' (I Cor. 1.19-27).

And now let us listen to the sound of Easter, which this Gospel record contains. Here the Evangelist describes how the elders stand and laugh, as people laugh when they have at last got rid of someone who had given them a good deal of trouble. Now He is finished. And the soldiers stand and laugh, because here once again it has been proved that four strong iron nails are much stronger than all religious discussion, and that it is far more sensible to stick to concrete real things than to religious dreams and illusions. This is now proved, and that is why they stand and laugh.

I want to ask you seriously, all of you who are coming to confess your sins: which of you has never joined in such laughter? Which of you would not then also have joined in this mockery? Which of you would have refused to join in the mockery solely out of a certain compassion, but not from any higher point of view?

Now, as you make your prayer of confession, reflect upon all your reasonable and clever resolutions, all your wise deeds and principles. Are they not in the long run simply a mockery of all His promises and warnings? Which of us will not now say: 'Lord, I, a poor, wretched, sinful man, confess that often in word and deed I have mocked at Thy Word, have held Thee to be weak and impotent, when Thou wast really all-powerful, and for a liar, when Thou hast told me the truth.' But Easter too is in the passage. They mock, and 'He that dwelleth in heaven shall laugh them to scorn: the Lord shall have them in derision' (Ps. 2.4). And since that day everyone of us may know that long ago the triumphant mockery of God has overcome the mockery of men. For in the Resurrection it becomes clear who was really right, who, really, was a caricature of a ruler—this despised Man hanging on the Cross, or the mighty Pilate who gave judgment, and at whom no one dared to laugh. Since that day anyone who sees this must never let himself be shocked by the wretchedness of Jesus Christ, by the misery of the Church, by the delay in the fulfilment of God's promises, but through all the mockery of his own heart he must range himself alongside this Man and say: 'Nevertheless I will remain with Thee.'

It is part of the mystery of the Passion story that in it, again and again, it is precisely in the mouths of the enemies of Jesus Christ that confessions are placed. Thus the high priest says: 'It is expedient for you that one man should die for the people' (John 11.50); and the Evangelist adds: 'He did not say this of his own accord, but being high priest that year he prophesied that Jesus should die for the nation.' Then Pilate says: 'I find no crime in Him'; and the Jews say: 'What need have we of further witness? We have heard it out of His own mouth.' And now those who stand beneath the Cross say, 'He saved others; Himself he cannot save.' The Evangelist is certainly of the opinion that this is a confession of Jesus Christ in the mouth of His enemies; for nothing else is more of the essence of Good Friday, than the fact that here God comes to us, not for His sake but for ours, that it is not Himself but others whom He saves. The world mocks where a man does this, but we rejoice and thank our Saviour.

This execution is one that no one can ever forget. There stand the three crosses. We know nothing about the previous life of the two men who hang on each side of the central Cross; but we know a great deal about the Man in the centre. And as we listen to the words which are being exchanged between them, we see that a shadow falls on the cross on the left, and that a light shines upon the one on the right. This means—for us all—that we are hanging on our crosses on either side of Jesus, and whichever side we are on, in some way or another, is due to our own choice. We now realise that at this moment, to which we have been called, all our previous life, our upbringing, the sins of our early life, and the sins which have brought us to death, do not matter in the least. Whether these two men who were hanging on either side of Jesus, were real murderers, or, as some commentators think, patriotic revolutionaries, whether their end was due to fate, or temperament, or to their own sins, whether their deeds were so very bad after all, or not—does not make an ounce of difference. All that lay behind them faded away, and their real decision became clear.

This comes out in one of the crucified in a very remarkable way. We cannot help being amazed at what is taking place within this man's heart: it is a vast change. We do not know when it began, perhaps at the moment when he heard the prayer which the Man at his side prayed: 'Father, forgive them, for they know not what they do.' Perhaps at this moment when the words penetrated his mind, in the midst of his own sufferings, for the first time he looked across to this Man, and *saw* Him. And then—it was a movement of the Holy Spirit—the scales fell from his eyes, and he saw Who He really was. And something took place within himself which is a veritable enigma. A man, a criminal, who is being executed, suddenly accepts his fate. 'We are receiving the due reward of our deeds.' For a man to be able to say this while he is dying in agony must be due to the fact that Jesus of Nazareth is hanging at his side.

So we come here tonight, and repeat after him this confession, which is the confession of us all: 'Lord, we are receiving the due reward of our deeds—remember us when You come in Your kingly power.' Before this, doubtless, this man had uttered curses and groans, and perhaps also prayers; but now, for the first time, he was really able to pray. If you are hanging on a cross, then you will curse, or you will cry out with sighs and groans, or even with prayers which seem to echo in a void. But you do not know whether anyone is there to hear your cries and prayers, or, even if there is someone, whether he is powerful enough to help you. But now Jesus Christ hangs alongside of you on the cross. Only then, but then quite surely, you *know*. Someone has heard, and He is not far away; here He is, at our side, and He has heard our prayer—and He is a King! 'Lord, remember me, when You come in Your kingly power.' That is the whole difference between a pagan prayer which is breathed out into the darkness, doubting and uncertain, and the prayer of a man who sees Jesus Christ. He sees a Jesus Who knows the same suffering! Jesus is bearing what you are bearing, and you say to Him: 'Lord, remember me.'

And the answer that Jesus gives is the miracle of grace and justification, which now takes place within you. Paradise, according to the view of the Jews of that period, was the place where the righteous, after their death, wait for the resurrection. It is the forecourt of the resurrection. When Jesus says to this man: 'Today, you, a criminal, will wait with me in the forecourt of the righteous for the resurrection,' this means: 'Now you are on the side of the righteous.' We approach Him and ask: 'Lord choose us, send down upon us

77

Thy Holy Spirit! We all hang on our own crosses, exposed
to heat and wind and weather. Sooner or later we shall all
draw our last breath. Lord, it is the mystery of Thine election
that upon one there falls the shadow and on the other light.
We do not know why in the one man a movement towards
God begins, while another remains dumb. "Then two men
will be in the field; one is taken and one is left" (Matt. 24.40).
Lord, for the sake of the Blood Thou hast shed for us, we pray
Thee: begin in us that movement which accepts all that Thou
dost lay upon us, which prays: "Lord remember me," and
then hears Thy word: "Today you still belong to the company of the righteous." '

Then, as you come to Holy Communion, you will be lifted
above all your doubts, and you will say with the dying thief:

> *My days are few, O fail not,*
>   *With Thine immortal power,*
> *To hold me that I quail not*
>   *In death's most fearful hour:*
> *That I may fight befriended,*
>   *And see in my last strife*
> *To me Thine arms extended*
>   *Upon the Cross of life.*

X

Luke 23.44-49

It was now about the sixth hour, and there was darkness over the whole land until the ninth hour, while the sun's light failed; and the curtain of the temple was torn in two.

Then Jesus, crying with a loud voice, said, 'Father, into Thy hands I commit My spirit!' And having said this He breathed His last.

Now when the centurion saw what had taken place, he praised God, and said, 'Certainly this Man was innocent!' And all the multitudes who assembled to see this sight, when they saw what had taken place, returned home, beating their breasts. And all His acquaintances, and the women who had followed Him from Galilee, stood at a distance and saw these things.

N o w the story of the way of the Cross is ended. The work has been completed; all that has happened is now final, with that bitter finality which we feel so acutely every time that we are confronted by the fact of death. There are no farewells upon earth in which we have not at least a very faint hope that it is not the last one, that it is not farewell for ever. Death alone—and this is what makes it so bitter for us when we stand by an open grave—is irrevocable. Here we know, so far as we can see with our human eyes, that there will be no *Wiedersehen;* once this has happened, nothing can be altered. Death makes us wholly responsible for our actions. Man's rejection of his Lord was final at the moment when Jesus literally breathed His last. We know very well—every Passiontide hymn says so—that it was not only the men of that day and of that nation who said 'No' : 'It is I who should repent.' And it is no accident that possibly all poetical efforts to describe a second coming of Christ upon earth in a different period, including the efforts of our own day, all end, finally, with the fact that they reject Him afresh, and put Him to death. We do not see Man in his reality save in the mirror of this story of the Passion. This story reveals the final truth about ourselves.

But the Passion story is not told with this end in view. It is only as it were in passing that our true nature is unveiled in such a way that it terrifies us. The guilt is mentioned only in passing, just as someone might speak of a sin which he had already forgiven. When we read this story of the Passion we may and can look upon this death as a help. Only those who are profoundly aware of the suffering of the world, it is true, find this a help. Holy Week and Passiontide, of this year 1940, when so much sorrow and pain surrounds us if we are attentive to what is happening, when we sometimes feel that it is almost more than we can bear, should not end without bringing us the help of Christ on His Cross for all the suffering in this world of ours.

The suffering of Christ points us away from our own suffering to the suffering of God for this world. The suffering of Christ is the deepest participation of God in this world. You must understand this, in order that this may really help you in your own suffering, and in your effort to share the pain of others; the suffering of Christ gives an awe-inspiring gravity to our life. It shows us that ultimately, at the root of all our suffering, is our sin. It is significant that when a paralysed man was brought to Jesus for healing His first word to the patient was not a word of sympathy, but a reminder of his sin : 'Man, your sins are forgiven you.' All human suffering is a reminder that we all cause God to suffer by our disloyalty, and the hardness of our hearts. The Cross of Christ shows us that God did not make it any easier for Himself than for us, but, on the contrary, that the hardest end has been borne by Him alone. Christ's way of the Cross was a way into a desolation which none of us can ever know, but which would have been our lot—the lot of us all—had Christ not trodden this way before us. The Cross of Christ is the sign of the separation between heaven and earth, which we could never grasp, but as it would have confronted us had not the Cross been erected by God Himself. As we try to understand this, as we realise what God's love had to suffer from our behaviour, and from our whole attitude towards Him, more and more we shall forget what we ourselves have to suffer.

That is one side of the subject; and the other is this. The Passion story has its own mystery, because it includes so many contradictory elements. For instance, immediately after the final word of desolation—that enigmatic saying implying that the Son of God is forsaken by God, according to the Gospels of Mark (15.34) and Matthew (27.46), which possibly was heard only by someone standing close to the Cross—comes the word of closest union with Him who lays this suffering upon Him. So He trod the way of the Cross, not thinking for a moment that all this was laid upon Him merely by the wicked world, by the Jews, by His enemies who hated Him, but in the firm knowledge that 'they could not do all this were it not the purpose of God, if it were not laid upon Me by the Father. This suffering is the Father's Cup which He hands to Me to drink!' And now, to Him who lays this upon Him; He says: 'Father.' This one word 'Father'—uttered by His Son in the extreme torture and agony of death, expresses more than any other word could convey of willing consent, of the inmost, heartfelt union of His will with the will of Him who permits Him to be put to death.

The fact that Jesus says this is an answer to all the questions which the sorrow of the world awakens in our impatient hearts, which are always too easily disturbed—to all the questions in your own life, and in the life of the people whom you now bring before God. He says, 'Father'. Unless He helps each of us to say 'Father' with Him, none of us can really bear our pain; we shall only drag it along behind us, until we break down. Without this 'Father' of Jesus Christ no one can really rise above his suffering. We may perhaps try to avoid it, or to run away from it; we may even try to get rid of it prematurely, but we shall not overcome it. That is—we cannot rise above it until we have extracted from it the blessing which this suffering conceals. Will it do you any good to run away from an experience of suffering, if you have not first of all shared in the blessing which it contains—which indeed was waiting for you in this pain? If you *were* successful in evading it, then you would be the poorer for it. We have no right to think, however, that in some way or another it was easier for Jesus to say this word 'Father' than it would be for us, who find it so impossibly difficult. We must face the fact that there is no other way out, no other real help in human suffering save this—that when we enter into this word 'Father', we accept from His hand all that is laid upon us, and all that will be laid upon us in the future. We accept it from the Father's hand; and we accept it willingly, looking only for the blessing which we believe this suffering contains.

This Word was uttered in the midst of tortures with which the world can make no comparison. Crucifixion itself is an inspiration of the devil, a method of execution which involves the very worst kind of refined and diabolic torture. The one who is crucified hangs on the cross, exposed to the heat of the sun; his wounds become inflamed; his whole body is already an open wound from the effects of the scourging; the body tends to become rigid so that in the midst of his pain he cannot move. In addition, the man on the cross suffered from an anguish worse than death, which was worse than all the other pain put together, and since he did not know when death would come, since he only knew that he was irretrievably on the way to death, the hours seemed endless. For Christ the physical suffering of crucifixion—in which He shared the

sufferings of all those who have ever died this death by crucifixion—was only the outward aspect of the inward conflict
which He endured; we can never know or imagine the extent
and depth of His spiritual suffering. Yet it was not just 'at any
time', but at *this* particular moment, that Jesus said, 'Father'.
So we see that it was not just at any time, but at the moment
of His greatest suffering, that He uttered, in our hearing, the
word 'Father'. This is no figure of speech. Jesus knows what
He means. He is sharing in all the suffering of the world, and
He shows us the way through : 'Father'.

What this means comes out in the fact that He adds a
phrase from the thirty-first Psalm. In so doing, the Crucified
Lord is expounding to us the meaning of the word 'Father'.
The fact that He chose a phrase from the Book of Psalms
shows, first of all, that in the presence of all who heard Him
praying these words, He was making a confession of faith. If
you read this Psalm—which is one of the most beautiful
Psalms—you will find that in it a righteous man is crying out
to God, full of confidence that God will protect him from all
the snares of his enemies. The fact that Jesus, who seemed
outwardly to be a man whom God had forsaken, used this
Psalm as a prayer, shows very clearly what was in His mind.
There is no shadow of doubt that He knew what His mission
was. It meant that, in every situation, this prayer of the
'righteous' man in Israel applied to Himself, and that in spite
of all that God was laying upon Him, He was perfectly sure
that God was His Protector. There He hangs, nailed to the
Cross, and the only room He has upon earth is one beam of
this cross of wood—and He is praying this Psalm which includes the words : 'Thou hast set my feet in a large room.'
When He prayed thus He was making a confession of His
Messiahship, and offering a thanksgiving for the revealed goodness of God in His own life.

Secondly, we note that Jesus did not here pray in His own
words. He did not offer a prayer which we might think was
applicable to Him alone. He was using a prayer which was

familiar to the Jews of His own day, one which everyone knew. Even if a Jew heard only one verse, he knew that count-less people in earlier ages had prayed this prayer in their troubles and sorrows. And so He takes part in *our* prayers. When you, in your own suffering, or in that of another, lift up your hands in prayer, you can be sure of this: Jesus Christ is taking part in your prayer. You are not alone, but He is speaking the same words with you. He enters wholly into your suffering.

This leads us directly to the third point. Literally, Jesus brings our prayer—since he prays it in His own suffering—before God. Thus no prayer which is offered in His Name, and claiming His sympathy, can ever fall to the ground. Apart from Him, our prayer would be a feeble breath, which could not rise through the clouds, and would lose itself in the mists. *With* Him, when He prays it, we may be sure that now no prayer can be unanswered, that it rises up to God: 'Father, into Thy hands I commend My spirit.' And as we hear Him praying with us, in *our* own words, we are also challenged to entrust everything to Him—to entrust to Him our body which is sick, our soul which we have injured; our children, the years we have wasted, the vocation we have missed, the mess we have made of our marriage, our failure as parents, our burdens and our sorrows. ' "Father", in the name of Jesus Christ I commit all these into Thy hands!' Do not think that this is impossible. Since Jesus Christ became Man, it has be-come quite possible, and every one of us can do it.

In order to show this, the Passion story ends with some-thing particularly beautiful. There, under the Cross, already stands the new Church. The Lord disappears from this life upon earth. He has been killed; 'His own People received Him not.' Pilate thinks: 'Now this case is really over.' The chief priests think. 'Now this tiresome man has been got rid of for good and all.' They do not seem to have troubled about the few disciples of Jesus; they did not arrest them because they probably thought: 'If the leader has died, the followers will soon be scattered and be forgotten.' But here, under the Cross, stands the new Church. It is scarcely aware of itself yet. It has no idea where or how to begin. Pain, disappointment, sorrow, fill their hearts with anguish, but they are *there*, gathered round the Cross, these men who only a little while ago had been scattered abroad. 'And all his acquaintances and the women who had followed Him from Galilee stood at a distance and saw these things.' Some at least of the rest of the Jewish people seem to have joined these followers of Jesus, for it is said of them that they 'returned home beating their breasts'. Thus, under the Cross, an inward movement had begun which would later lead them to listen to the words of the Apostles, which would pierce their hearts, lead them to repent, and to come home to the Father. Finally, as the representative of us all, the representative of the pagan world, comes the centurion. Legend calls him Longinus. He says that this Man who has just died on the cross was never a criminal —He had always been a good Man. That is, He had been not a criminal, not One who is on the side of the sinner, but One who belongs to the side of God. This officer was the first of a stream of countless men and nations from the pagan world who have come to the Cross on pilgrimage. Among them is our own nation. It has been incorporated into this new Church, and thus it too has been enabled to enter into a new experience—to discover that in the depth of sorrow and distress we can say 'Father', and so we can bear all the suffering we have to bear, and we can overcome it. Those who will not come under this Cross and confess Jesus as their Lord will not find it possible to bear the suffering and to overcome. Therefore we beseech Him, the Crucified Lord, to 'abide with us, for it is toward evening, and the day is far spent.'[1] 'We commit to Thee this nation, the whole human family, our life and all our pains and sorrows—into thy hands.'

[1] From the evening prayer of the German Lutherans (*Translator*).

XI

Luke 23.50-56

Now there was a man named Joseph, from the Jewish town of Arimathea. He was a member of the council, a good and righteous man,
who had not consented to their purpose and deed, and he was looking for the kingdom of God. This man went to Pilate and asked for
the body of Jesus. Then he took it down and wrapped it in a linen
shroud, and laid Him in a rock-hewn tomb, where no one had ever
yet been laid. It was the day of Preparation, and the sabbath was
beginning. The women who had come with Him from Galilee followed,
and saw the tomb, and how His body was laid; then they returned,
and prepared spices and ointments.

O N Good Friday the world came to an end. Nothing more
could happen. Good Friday is the end of the world, because
all human self-sufficiency, and indeed also all confidence in
human gifts and talents, have broken down. When in the
creed we say, 'He suffered under Pontius Pilate, was crucified,
dead, and buried', we should be quite clear about this: this
ancient formula is saying the most terrible thing that could
ever be said. It confirms, as with a seal, the hopelessness of
the world. Now the world has rejected even this final hope.
And we have come so far that the final offer has been rejected.
Now we have reached the extreme limit of all our human
possibilities. *Nothing* more is possible. World history may of
course continue; but there is no longer any meaning, any

future, any hope. That is what the word in the creed means: *buried*.

In this closing section of the Passion story, in the account of the burial of Jesus, the figure of Joseph of Arimathea comes like a distant echo, like a faint suggestion of promise. Something may still be going to happen; there is a dim hope that, though the world has come to an end, God has not come to an end; there is a dawning hope that great changes may be imminent. Luke the Evangelist says that Joseph was a good man, who had not 'consented to their purpose and deed'—that is, to the sentence given by the chief priests and the scribes, and that he was a man who 'was looking for the Kingdom of God'. So Joseph was a man who was waiting for something, not one who thought he already possessed what he desired, but who was full of expectation, based upon a certain promise. This is why he did not reject this Jesus of Nazareth, although in this he was unlike the rest of the people who were also waiting for something or someone. For the Pharisees and the scribes were also waiting; but they thought they knew what they were waiting for, and indeed they had already decided beforehand what it would be. As we read the New Testament we cannot remind ourselves too often how repellent, how devastating, was the appearance of Jesus Christ to these religious people. It was contrary to all their expectations. His deeds, His words, His behaviour, the company he kept—all contradicted their own ideas and ideals. They were very religious people, perhaps a good deal more than we are today. And how horrified we would all have been by this Jesus of Nazareth!

Joseph of Arimathea was a man who knew how to wait. Because he did not lay down beforehand what God would do, but only held out his hands and desired the fulfilment of the promise, he saw more in this Jesus than all the scribes and Pharisees could see. Since he *was* still waiting, it is clear that he was also a very disappointed man. His expectations had not been fulfilled. The One on Whom his hopes were set had been executed. As night fell on that day of horror, the bodies of the executed men gleaned on their crosses with a ghostly light. And where Jesus had been, where there had been hope, there was now only a corpse. The hope of the Kingdom of God had become a corpse.

But again, there is now a faint suggestion of dawning light in the darkness, in the fact that there seems to have been a change in this man, Joseph of Arimathea. John the Evangelist says that he had been a disciple of Jesus, but only 'secretly for fear of the Jews'. Probably he was one of those men who had been profoundly despised by the disciples of Jesus because they had not had the courage to confess their adherence to this Jesus of Nazareth openly, and had not fearlessly surrendered everything in order to become his disciples. Joseph of Arimathea was a timid, secret, bad disciple. He believed in the secrecy of his heart, but dared not confess with his lips. And now, when all Christ's disciples had fled, when all who had openly professed their loyalty to Him had forsaken Him, and left Him alone, a great change has taken place in this timid, reticent man. He is now full of courage—and it must have taken some courage to show himself on the side of a Man Who had been cast out and executed. Now, less than ever, could we expect anyone to stand up for Him. Yet at this very moment, suddenly, something flared up within him. Probably he could scarcely have said whence he drew the strength to take this step, any more than did Nicodemus, who, as St John records, accompanied Joseph on his courageous visit to Pilate, in order to ask for the body of Jesus. Nicodemus had recognised Jesus as the Master, who 'comes from God'. But he had only dared to visit Him secretly, by night. And now when all who were known to be His disciples and followers had been scattered, and not one of them dared to come out of hiding, then the Holy Spirit roused two timid people, poor secret disciples, and it is they who openly proclaimed themselves on the side of Jesus, in order that they might be allowed to remove His body from the Cross.

'He took it down', we read. That is a terrible phrase. For Joseph and for all those who were with him, it was a terrible moment. With what emotions must they have been filled as they drew the nails out of His hands and feet, as they let down the body from the Cross, as they saw the mouth which had spoken the words of eternal life, now closed and silent, as they saw the eyes which were once streaming with love and light, now sightless in death! Now He is dead—finally. And in order to confirm this finality He is laid in the grave, in a cave in the rock, hollowed out like a room, and then a great stone is rolled up against the entrance. And then, the writer adds, as a gentle reminder that this was a very special person and a very special corpse, and a very special hope which was being buried, that 'no one before this had lain in this grave'.

If one of you, during the previous year, even perhaps during this Passiontide, has stood by a grave, you will know, and have a very keen recollection of the fact, that this word in the creed, 'buried', is not superfluous. Do not we all know what it means when we carry a dead person to the grave? So long as the coffin is in the house, and the dead body is still there, we feel as though he were still there, as though he had not quite gone away. And then, when the coffin is lowered into the grave, and the earth receives it, then comes the final break, then it is indeed 'all over'. So this word 'buried' here expresses something final, something irrevocable, and irremovable. Now it is over. Now the world has succeeded in putting God behind its back, in making God as 'past' as a dead body. 'God's Son is dead.' The world has no more to do with Him. But with this death, their own hope too has vanished. At this grave all hope has vanished. All that led up to it is like a tale that is told: 'Once upon a time . . .' Where the world is concerned, it is all over with Jesus—and thus with God. 'Dost Thou show wonders among the dead?' asks a Psalmist, and, before his own death comes, he beseeches God to make an end of death and burial, and not destroy all hope. And yet God did allow death to occur. As with the young man at Nain, as with Lazarus, so now with Jesus, death is finally master. Where then is God's power and sovereignty? 'Dost Thou show wonders among the dead: or shall the dead rise up again, and praise Thee? Shall Thy loving-kindness be shewed in the grave: or Thy faithfulness in destruction?' (Ps. 88.10-11). The universal answer to the Psalmist's question is 'No'. There is no remedy for death. In death all is *dead*. And yet the same Christ who now is dead and buried had on the day before, on the evening of Maundy Thursday when He instituted the Eucharist (as we read in the Gospel of Mark), *sung a song of praise*. This praise consisted, according to Jewish custom, of parts of Psalms 113-118. And if we open these Psalms this evening we can read in them one Resurrection saying after another. 'Right dear in the sight of the Lord is the death of His saints' (Ps. 116.13). 'I shall not die, but live: and declare the works of the Lord' (Ps. 118.17). *Non moriar sed vivam*. Who then is right? Jesus, with His song of praise? or His grave? Will God even do wonders among the dead? Will the dead rise again, and praise Him? Yes, they will: it *will* happen!

Christoph Blumhardt once said that we ought to weep at Christmas, because then God is giving so much away, because God is coming into the world in sacrifice; but on Good Friday we ought to laugh; for then God is bringing the world back to Himself. And since He went down into the deepest depths, into the irrevocable hopelessness of those who are dead and buried, then 'He calls into existence the things that do not exist' (Rom. 4.17). That is the message of Good Friday.

Henceforth from this One Who was buried there falls upon our own death a great shadow and a radiant light. *A shadow* —for this we learn in the death of Jesus Christ: he who is dead is really, irrevocably, *dead*. Death in itself is not, as our poets would like to think, a fulfilment. It is a tearing away, a breakdown, a condemnation, which makes all life lose its meaning. It is 'the wages of sin'. *A bright light*—for here we learn for our own death, from the death of Jesus, the song of

90

praise: 'I shall not die but live.' When we go into the grave with Him, with Christ Himself, we are not alone—there, where man is so utterly alone, and so lonely. One has lain before us in our own grave, and He will lift the lid and roll away the stone of hopelessness and finality. Through Him those who die do really rise again and praise God. Through Him graves really do become places where God's goodness and faithfulness are praised. *Jesus lives!* we now sing:

> *henceforth is death*
> *But the gate of life immortal.*

So our hopelessness becomes a preparation for a hope, our grave a sign of life—because even in the grave we have communion with Jesus Christ. For there He lies too. And now we know—and if you think it is incredible, in the Holy Communion you are assured by the Risen, Living Lord: 'You belong to Me, even in the grave.' And when He makes a promise He always keeps His word. We shall not die, but live, and declare the works of the Lord.

XII

Luke 24.1-12

But on the first day of the week, at early dawn, they went to the tomb, taking the spices which they had prepared. And they found the stone rolled away from the tomb, but when they went in they did not find the body. While they were perplexed about this, behold, two men stood by them in dazzling apparel; and as they were frightened and bowed their faces to the ground, the men said unto them, 'Why do you seek the living among the dead? Remember how He told you, while He was still in Galilee, that the Son of Man must be delivered into the hands of sinful men, and be crucified, and on the third day rise.' And they remembered His words, and returning from the tomb they told all this to the eleven and to all the rest.

Now it was Mary Magdalene and Joanna and Mary the mother of James and the other women with them, who told this to the apostles; but these words seemed to them an idle tale, and they did not believe them. But Peter rose and ran to the tomb; stooping and looking in, he saw the linen cloths by themselves; and he went home wondering what had happened.

A CHURCH was already there, to which the first Resurrection message could come. It was already there, just as it still is here today—and in many places it is certainly 'there' in exactly the same way as it was then. The people come together, they pray together, they keep the sabbath and celebrate the Passover, and the feasts of the Church. But this is a weak and miserable affair; it changes nothing in the world; it causes no upheaval. What is it that holds this group together? Perhaps a little loyalty to their cause? Many people, indeed, have a fine trait in their character : even when they think they are supporting a lost cause, they do not at once give it up and turn to something which might be more profitable. Even when it seems to be a forlorn hope, they still stick to it, possibly very courageously, but perhaps also with a dash of fatalism as well. We can indeed respect and sympathise with people of such strong character; but they cannot win others through their own experience. This kind of loyalty did, doubtless, hold this Church together—and in addition there was also the wealth of memories, the common tradition of those years of companionship with Jesus. When we look at the motives which affect people even today, we see that very often it is this kind of tradition which, to a large extent, still holds the Church together. It holds many of *you* to the Church —fidelity to this idea, even when you no longer expect very much from it, and the remembrance of what this Church has meant to your fathers, and perhaps even in your own lives. This is all quite good in its way, but at bottom it does not mean anything; it has no power, and so far as the world is concerned, it is neither a danger nor a help.

The authorities of that day were quite right in thinking that this community, which was held together only by a little loyalty and tradition, was not even worth the trouble of a proper persecution. Some of the religious leaders may even have thought: 'Such people deserve respect and sympathy. They have some fine ideas, and a great inheritance. But this does not alter the fact that the whole affair is unimportant. There is no need to bother about it any more. It is bound to die out of itself.'[1]

It was into such a Church that this news came, and indeed it burst upon them, then as now. It is not at all surprising that at first they could hardly believe it. Many among you, if you had been living then, would have believed it as little as you

[1] The 'German Christians' tolerated, and were tolerated by, the Nazis (*Translator*).

believe it today. You too regard this message of the Resurrection merely as an ancient, respected dogma, even if you do not dare to doubt it. But if we were to talk about it frankly and privately, many of you would finally confess that fundamentally you would feel like the disciples of those days : 'It's all fairy tales—women's gossip!' 'And they did not believe them.' When the Apostle Paul was in pagan Athens, the Athenians laughed him to scorn when he mentioned the Resurrection of Jesus Christ; they thought he was telling them something completely 'mad'. The first messengers of the Resurrection had exactly the same experience, when they brought the message to Christ's own disciples in the heart of the Church of Christ. Thus we have no right to be indignant with the unbelieving world. For in the midst of the Church the message of the Resurrection was received as something totally incredible. Why was this? The two men in dazzling garments say it quite plainly. The weakness, sadness, and impotence of the Church—its unbelief, with regard to the message of the Resurrection—all this was due to the fact that they were seeking 'the Living among the dead'.

When we read in the Gospels, frequently, that the disciples of Jesus did not 'understand', it does not mean that their minds could not rise to it. Their lack of understanding consisted in the fact that, at bottom, they were seeking Jesus among the dead—that is, they thought He still belonged to the world of the dead, although even in Galilee, in the early days of His ministry, He had told them what would happen, that ultimately everything would end in the great victory of God in the midst of the world of death. The disciples could not 'understand', because although in theory they believed that God was the Lord of the world, *actually* they thought that He was only the Lord above, in heaven, but that here upon earth everything and everyone, even Jesus Himself, was in the grip of death's power. Because they believed this, their faith remained simply an ideal. So, just as many people do nowadays, they turned reality into a beautiful idea. But when men or women do this, immediately they lose their distinction from the rest of the world as Christian disciples. With the rest of the world they then share the common unshakable belief in the power of death, the conviction that the course of this world, with its empire of death, can never be changed, and that this means that upon earth God Himself is powerless. So long as the disciples believed this, they were neither a danger nor a help to this world; and so long as any of you believe like this, actually your whole Christianity means nothing. The one thing that matters for the Church is that she should be both a danger and a help to the world.

It was with this aim that the Easter story broke into our world, bringing with it a power, a world-overcoming revolution, which makes everything different in our life, which forces the Church into a totally different direction. When this message came to the disciples, they could no longer be a 'Church' in the previous sense. Something fundamentally different took its place. And it is the same with the Church today: she also must become totally different. This message alone can make things really different. Here and there, today, it is already a little different—that is, people begin to realise that it is not enough to go on celebrating Easter as before, and to go on living as though God were only a beautiful idea, and a nice traditional conception for Sunday mornings, and as if otherwise everything else in the world will always go on in the same old way. Without this message of Easter, unbelief reigns in the midst of the Church so that people are not prepared for it, but like Peter, at most they 'wonder' when God's reality touches them, and they begin to discover that God is a living God, not a 'painted', dead one.

'Why do you seek the Living among the dead?' The women who heard this knew at once who was meant by 'the Living One'. This one word was sufficient to reawaken within them all that Jesus of Nazareth had meant to them. Why did they follow Him? For Whose sake had they left everything? Why had they no other desire than to be with Him? Why was this?

Was it not because in the words and deeds of Jesus, and indeed in His whole personality, they realised that the power of the divine life was present, that it was with them in the midst of their life, in a way which they had never known before? They knew that this life was truth and love itself, and, although they could not express this, they knew that this life flowed from God—and not only so, but that *here and now* the life of God Himself was present. This meant that *here*, in the midst of our poor dark world, a light had dawned, kindled by God Himself; a power had come upon us which no demon could resist; a hope had been born, which meant that nothing was ever hopeless any more. Did they not feel that they could apply to this Man the words of the Psalmist: 'With Thee is the well of life; and in Thy light shall we see light' (Ps. 36.9)? When the angels asked this question, the disciples felt that they were asking them: 'Have you not noticed that His whole life and His whole being is *life* itself? It is unthinkable that He could possibly belong to death. Did you not notice how strange it sounded when, at the close of the Last Supper, He sang with you this Psalm of praise: "I shall not die, but live: and declare the works of the Lord" (Ps. 118.17)? Didn't you notice it?' Ah, yes, the women and the disciples had all noticed it. The angels only needed to pronounce the word 'the Living' to reawaken within them all their memories. As the presence of the divine life upon earth they had known Him, and that was why they followed Him. But at the same time this re-awakened within them the pain of these days, the pain of the terrible contradiction that He Whom they had known as the Living One had actually given up the ghost before their very eyes, and His battered body had been laid in the grave as a corpse. Even at the present day, the question of the angels arouses this sense of contradiction. Have you experienced that, even today, with this Jesus of Nazareth? Have you recognised that He is the Living One? This question challenges the faith of us all. 'Could you then really think,' the angels asked them, and all the messengers of the Resurrection ask this, and so I

96

ask it of you here today, 'could you really believe that in this matter, in which God has proved Himself so incomparably present, the end could finally be the end of all flesh, that the last word in this matter rests with death? Must you judge everything only by your human standards and your human possibilities? Have you so little faith in the power of God, and so uncanny a respect for the power of death, that you think, since this Man lies dead before your eyes, that His mission has failed, and that God is satisfied to let this happen? Why then does the Christ of God accept this contradiction? Why then did it happen that He, Who could not die, died a real and terrible death? Surely, the answer is not that He *is* dead, so that nothing and no one, not even God Himself, can resist the power of death? His purpose was rather that you, His disciples, should pass through this terrible experience—in order that you might know, once for all, that the Living is *not* among the dead, that the Living God has triumphed, even over death itself.

'And they remembered His words.' Everything that they had previously received from Him now sprang to life again. These vital words enabled them to receive the Resurrection faith into their hearts. Jesus Himself has to come with His words, and touch our hearts, and bring it into an eternal movement, and open our eyes, in order that we may know God's living Presence. Only then does the certainty of the Resurrection come into our hearts. The empty tomb might be explained in other ways—the chief priests were, indeed, very quick to spread a lie which helped them out of their embarrassment (Matt. 28.11-15). The two angels could also be represented as a hallucination of excited women—as, indeed, the disciples were inclined to believe at first. But when we know Jesus as the Living One, we are able to link His words, spoken earlier, with the Empty Tomb and with the message of the angels. The one confirms the other, and they are inseparably united.

How it happened remains shrouded in mystery. No one saw

the Resurrection. If anyone says 'This is impossible!' he is
saying nothing new. He is only saying what the Bible em-
phasises. It was no easier for Peter and Paul than for a modern
scientist to believe that this Jesus who was dead is alive. No
one can even imagine what happened, for it took place in the
night of the mystery of God, hidden from human eyes. What
our senses perceive is first of all the proclamation of Jesus,
and then the proclamation of the Resurrection by the angels;
all that lies between is the night of the divine miracle, the
night of faith.

In this night a complete transformation took place. If this
message is not to fall on deaf ears, no one ought to go out
from this church tonight without becoming, to some extent,
aware of this transformation. The change consists in the fact
that that which was certain has become doubtful, and that
which was doubtful has become very sure. A deadly doubt
entered the hearts of the disciples at that grave. It was perhaps not a doubt about the truth of the Person, Jesus Christ—
we are told nothing about that. But possibly it was a different
and more sinister doubt—whether the promise of God, which
for them had been fulfilled in this Man, was still operative. Was
there any hope left for this world which had rejected God? Had
God now left this world to itself, to death and hell? Had
things come to such a pass upon this earth that it was subject
only to the terrible law of death? After all, is not all our life
simply a journey towards death?

If this be so, then who inherits it all—our achievements and
our virtues and our successes, in the life of the individual as
well as in the life of nations? Is it not death, the great heir of
all things? Death's influence over us is so great that we are
not only cut down like corn in a harvest field at death—even
now death dominates our thoughts. Everything we do is an
effort to protect ourselves against death, and in so doing we
turn everything we touch into death. Is not this preoccupation
with death a horrible thing? The fact is that in every natural
gift, in every discovery, man does not first of all try to find

98

out what boon it offers, but concentrates on trying to discover the element of death which it contains, and then tries to change it into death, into a weapon of death. Is not that horrible? A deadly doubt crept into the hearts of the disciples: since God Himself had been rejected, was not this world finally a sacrifice to death? Is it not after all the case that sin and Satan actually have the last word, and that the power and grace of God are valid only in heaven, not among us, here upon earth? If we look at the Cross of Christ apart from the Resurrection, then it is sealed with a sentence of death, which once for all confirms the hopelessness of the world. But if we look at the Cross of Christ in the light of the Resurrection, then already Good Friday is the great day of God's victory, and not the day of death.

This question, 'Does God's hope for the world still hold good?', received a sure and positive answer in the Resurrection. This is one source of the power of the Church to transform the world. On the other hand, that which used to seem certain became doubtful. All of us who are Christians have to wrestle through to the point where that which used to be doubtful becomes certain. But if any one is not yet a Christian, or thinks he is not, he should first of all consider how that which until now he has regarded as utterly certain has become quite doubtful in the light of Easter. He must immediately become uncertain whether, as everybody at bottom believes, death really is the end of everything. A few days ago, in a lecture on the present religious situation, I heard it said that on the basis of all contemporary views of life the only possible conviction is this: 'Let us eat and drink, for tomorrow we die.' That is the certain dogma of modern man—that everything else is uncertain, but that death is certain. But we now begin to doubt the truth of this dogma. This is an 'Easter doubt' which steals into our hearts, bringing joy and confidence with it. Now we do *not* believe in the sovereignty of death upon earth, nor in the hopelessness of human life, nor that the course of this world can never be changed! We also reject the dogma that God is too mysterious and distant to be known; that the changefulness of life is a reason for sadness, or that pain has no meaning! Nor do we believe that might is stronger than right, and deceit stronger than truth! This kind of 'doubt' is full of joy. It is not based upon an optimistic view of life, which could easily be shattered. It is God-given, for it springs from the reality of Easter.

If we want to come into contact with Jesus without the Resurrection, we shall be 'perplexed'. The world indeed is always 'perplexed', because it regards Jesus as dead and it yet cannot find Him in His grave. On the contrary, it constantly becomes aware of signs of His life, which it finds most enigmatic. And when the Church allows herself to be led astray by the world, and tries to seek the Living among the dead, she too will become 'perplexed'. Oh! you who are 'perplexed' like this—even within the Church—if you will only let yourselves hear the Resurrection message from a couple of bewildered women, or from a few insignificant witnesses of Jesus Christ, then at once the sun will rise for you! When the Bolsheviks were about to shoot a Russian bishop, as he stood against the wall, and the order to fire had just been given, he called out: 'Farewell, you who are dead! I am going into life!' In this life you now stand. Jesus Christ the Living One is wholly present, oh! you 'perplexed' Church. Why do you seek the Living, and your own life, still among the dead?

XIII

Luke 24.13-35

That very day two of them were going to a village named Emmaus, about seven miles from Jerusalem, and talking with each other about all these things that had happened. While they were talking and discussing together, Jesus Himself drew near and went with them. But their eyes were kept from recognising Him. And He said to them, 'What is this conversation which you are holding with each other as you walk?' And they stood still, looking sad.

Then one of them, named Cleopas, answered Him, 'Are you the only visitor to Jerusalem who does not know the things that have happened there in these days?' And He said to them, 'What things?' And they said to Him, 'Concerning Jesus of Nazareth, Who was a prophet mighty in deed and word before God and all the people, and how our chief priests and rulers delivered Him up to be condemned to death, and crucified Him. But we had hoped that He was the One to redeem Israel. Yes, and besides all this, it is now the third day since this happened. Moreover, some women of our company amazed us. They were at the tomb early in the morning and did not find His body; and they came back saying that they had even seen a vision of angels, who said that He was alive. Some of those who were with us went to the tomb, and found it just as the women had said; but Him they did not see.' And He said to them, 'O foolish men, and slow of heart to believe all that the prophets have spoken! Was it not necessary that the Christ should suffer these things and enter into His glory?' And beginning with Moses and all the prophets, He interpreted to them in all the scriptures the things concerning Himself.

So they drew near to the village to which they were going. He appeared to be going further, but they constrained Him saying, 'Stay with us, for it is toward evening and the day is now far spent.' So He went in to stay with them. When He was at table with them, He took the bread and blessed, and broke it, and gave it to them. And

their eyes were opened and they recognised Him; and He vanished
out of their sight. They said to each other, 'Did not our hearts burn
within us while He talked to us on the road, while He opened to us
the scriptures?' And they rose that same hour and returned to Jerusalem; and they found the eleven gathered together and those who
were with them, who said, 'The Lord has risen indeed, and has
appeared to Simon!'

Then they told what had happened on the road, and how He was
known to them in the breaking of the bread.

T H E Y saw Him as He took the bread, as He broke it, and then
gave it to them. They had often seen Him do this. But now,
as this Stranger did it, it must have immediately reminded
them of one particular evening when these two, Cleopas and
the other disciple, were not present, of which they had only
heard from the apostles. When they saw this Stranger do this,
that evening, that last evening flashed before their eyes. And
then they *knew* Him.

Why had they not recognised Him before? This seems to
have been just as enigmatic for the Evangelist, as well as for
those who experienced it, as it is to us who read about it.
Perhaps one reason was the fact that they would not have
considered it possible that it could be He. Perhaps there was
a certain heavenly atmosphere about Him which was strange
to them, and possibly even His face, which was included in
His glorification, made Him look different from the Man they
had hitherto known. But all this is only a 'perhaps'. All that
the Evangelist says is this: 'Their eyes were kept from recognising him.' In any case, in spite of the way their hearts had
burned within them as they listened to His conversation,
they still did not recognise Him. Evidently they were not
meant to recognise Him yet. Evidently He Himself chose the
moment when they would be able to know Him. This is
entirely His affair; when anyone *does* recognise Him, in this
act of recognition he receives the gift of Christ. That is why

neither of these two disciples knew Him until the Stranger did what the Lord had done at the Last Supper : 'He took the bread, gave thanks, brake it, and gave to them.'

Quite deliberately, the Evangelist, as he tells the story, uses the same words which have already been used in the story of the Last Supper. Through this supper with the disciples at Emmaus, a bridge had been thrown unexpectedly over the gulf which yawned between what had happened before the Crucifixion, and what would be from now until the end of the world. That previous meal was a farewell supper, a final one, and Jesus had emphasised this when He said continually 'no more'. 'For I tell you I shall not eat it until it is fulfilled in the Kingdom of God' (Luke 22.16-18). That last meal was strictly in the past; for after that came death. We never see more clearly that we are human beings, for whom the present is always becoming an irrevocable past, than when we stand by a death-bed, a coffin, or an open grave. Then we know : something is over and finished for good. Of course this is happening hour after hour, but we are not so conscious of it. This winter is over; we did live in a time of peace, but that is past; you have experienced this and that, you have gone through this or that trouble and anxiety, but now it is past. We are now in a time of war, but sometime or another that too will become the past. But what it really means to be 'past' becomes actual for us in death. So Jesus had become a past figure (someone who *had* been) when He hung on the cross; and when the stone blocked the entrance to the grave it was also the stone that sealed off the past, irrevocably, from the present. 'Never again shall we eat and drink with Him!' And now He was here, and He was eating and drinking with them! This means simply : now, they are drawn into that Last Supper. Now, so to speak, His last hour before the end *expands*, and takes into itself all the hours that are to come, which the Church can now experience upon earth. It embraces within itself the disciples, just as these two disciples have now been taken into the circle of the Apostles. And this will be for the whole Church—*all* will be included.

The fact that the Last Supper can be repeated is not something which can be taken for granted. Nor can it be taken for granted that the Supper can be administered not only by the apostles, but now also by us Christians who have been appointed to do so by the Church. It presupposes that a bridge has been thrown across the deep gulf which was made by the Cross—that a link has been fashioned between what Jesus was before the Crucifixion to His disciples, and what He wills to be to us all, down to the present day. His last 'hour' has expanded to infinity. The whole course of this world, during these past two thousand years, and the few hundreds or thousands of years which God now allows to be extending before us until He makes an end of this earth—all that will be gathered into the last hour. 'Children, it is the last hour,' writes the Apostle (I John 2.18). Hence we celebrate the Last Supper in the Eucharist as those who share in it, and the 'breaking of bread' at Emmaus draws us all into the Church of the apostles. That is why, henceforth, the gravity of death and the radiance of resurrection brood over every Eucharist that we celebrate. 'And they knew Him.' The Eucharist is the place where great knowledge is given to us. At the time of the Reformation it was called *signum certitudinis*, the sign and pledge of certainty. So if any of you are confused and afraid and tempted, you should come to Communion. If you do not know Jesus, but you want to know Him, if you do not notice that Jesus has already been walking with you for a long time, you should come to Communion. For a promise broods over this hour, the promise that here Christ can be known in His living presence.

But—and you should note this very carefully—all this had a history that led up to it. These two men were not a couple of pagans who were at once received into the Church, a couple of men who were strangers to Christ, and who only now had come into contact with Him. Rather, the supper at Emmaus is the feast of recognition for those who have already had a previous history of contact with Christ. This previous history is twofold. It consists in a great hope, and in a great disappointment. 'But we *had hoped* that He was the one to redeem Israel.' Both these men who sat at table with Him, had shared in the greatest hope which has ever existed upon earth —that is, the history of the people of Israel. To deny the Old Testament, and the people of Israel, without seeing this hope, is like a blind person who complains of a colour he has never seen.[1] Anyone who has really seen and understood the hope which entered into the hearts of the men of the Old Testament, regards the rest of world history as a hopeless and aimless affair. From within world history there arises this history of Israel, as the history of a deathless hope. It is the hope of a deliverance that will come, when the world will be lifted out of its lost condition, when the bonds which fetter mankind will be severed, and death and the devil will be deprived of their power. Things will not always go on in the same old way; redemption is sure, and all history is moving towards a great act of redemption by God Himself. That was the hope on which those men lived, and it was never so alive and ardent as in the days when Jesus walked this earth among His people—'a prophet mighty in deed and word before God, and before all this people'.

These two men said: 'We *had* hoped.' They implied that this hope died when Christ died. But they did not mean that Jesus had disappointed them. They were not expressing a doubt about Jesus. It would be a great mistake to think that what they were saying is 'We placed our hope in a name that has proved an illusion.' No, what they mean is this: 'This Man *was* the right Man, but our chief priests and rulers delivered Him up to be condemned to death, and crucified Him.' That was the greatest assault on their faith which they could possibly have had to endure. The doubt whether God really exists, and whether Jesus had really told the truth—those are

[1] An attack on Nazi anti-Semitism is implied here (*Translator*).

still quite minor temptations. The really great temptation is only experienced by a man who, standing in the midst of this history of a hope, who has thus become a man of hope, has no more doubts about God and Jesus Christ, but who feels the greatest and final doubt of all creeping into his mind: namely that Jesus had perhaps long ago revoked His promise, that He has allowed Himself to be rejected by us, that He has finished with us. So when anyone here comes to confession, he confesses that he can conceive that God *could* do this; and he says that this is what causes him so much distress, more than all the other evil in the world. It is the final temptation, to be afraid that God has cast us off, that He has 'finished' with us.

So as these two disciples walked that day along the country road, they were feeling this disappointment which bordered on despair; they were not disappointed in Jesus, but with themselves and the whole world. And perhaps the most glorious thing in this whole story is what happens before they recognise Him. At the very moment that a person is in the deepest distress of mind, Jesus has been already walking with him for a long time. Then you understand how it is that men who have had such experiences are lifted above their former fears. Henceforth nothing can 'get them down'—neither disappointment, nor trial, nor temptation. For now they know for certain that it may *look* as though we are wholly forsaken; it may look as though we ourselves have destroyed our own dearest hopes; it may seem as though God had turned away His face from us; it may even seem as though for us, Christ no longer existed at all; it may seem as though Jesus and His Word and the Holy Scriptures have ceased to have any meaning for us—to have 'gone dead on us'; it may *seem* as though no hope is left; yes, it *may* look like that—but in reality, all the time, Jesus has been with us, walking at our side. He is not far off! He stands in the midst of us, listening to our prayers—bringing us His peace!

The Emmaus story, and the Holy Eucharist which we are

now about to celebrate, speak to our hearts, very simply, to us as we are, in all our distress, our sense of being forsaken, and our hopelessness. Don't be afraid! Be at rest—not in a spirit of passive resignation, not as though there were nothing more to hope for, but because, in spite of everything, the hope is still there, living and already fulfilled! Since the Cross of Calvary the hour of fulfilment has dawned for the world. Brothers, it is the last hour.

XIV

Luke 24.36-49

As they were saying this, Jesus Himself stood amongst them. But they were startled and frightened, and supposed that they saw a spirit. And He said to them, 'Why are you troubled, and why do questionings arise in your hearts? See My hands and My feet, that it is I Myself; handle Me, and see; for a spirit has not flesh and bones as you see that I have.' And while they yet disbelieved for joy, and wondered, He said to them, 'Have you here anything to eat?' They gave Him a piece of broiled fish, and He took it and ate it before them.

Then said He to them, 'These are my words which I spoke to you, while I was still with you, that everything written about Me in the law of Moses and the prophets and the psalms must be fulfilled.' Then He opened their minds to understand the scriptures, and said to them, 'Thus it is written, that the Christ should suffer and on the third day rise from the dead, and that repentance and forgiveness of sins should be preached in His name to all nations, beginning from Jerusalem. Ye are witnesses of these things. And behold, I send you the promise of My Father upon you; but stay in the city, until you are clothed with power from on high.'

A<small>ND</small> so we are living today on the fact that, at that particular time, these things happened. Take this little scene, this insignificant little incident, which took place in some unknown house in Jerusalem two thousand years ago, in a gathering of quite unknown and unimportant persons—'unimportant', that is, in the opinion of the rest of the world, if the world had even known of their existence. Take this unimpressive incident out of your own life—and nothing that matters is left, nothing at all. For from that moment, because of these 'incidents', there arose a movement which cannot be compared with any other movement. It is a revolution, compared with which all the other revolutions in the world are mere child's play. It is a movement which, as no other has ever done, has penetrated into the inmost history of mankind, without which no one today can think rightly about life, Man, and God. It is a movement apart from which no one can build his house of life (in spite of every effort to free himself from it). It is a movement, apart from which the history of Europe, and of the rest of the world, cannot be conceived. Everything else can be conceived as unnecessary, but not this one movement. And yet at bottom the immense historical results of these 'unimportant' incidents are really far less important than the results of these 'incidents', so long ago, in the personal life, and the inmost soul, of every man or woman who has listened to and obeyed their message. For this story has penetrated men's minds and hearts, challenging them to commit themselves— for or against. It gives hope where there was despair! No story of the past can be imagined which is so mysteriously 'present' as the story we read in these few verses.

And all this is only due to the fact that since those events took place the world has been open to the influence of witness to an actual fact. All that happened was the *fact* that as Jesus said, these people were witnesses: 'You are witnesses of these things.' This means that, after that hour, the first Christians saw that the main work of their life was to go into all the world, going ever further afield, to tell the story of what they had seen—as though in Macedonia, and in Rome, and everywhere else, there was nothing more important than to hear this story. And so they went everywhere, telling this story, in such a way that through that event each individual heard an unparalleled call. This story changes your life, turns your life upside down—as we learn that it is a word of repentance and of forgiveness. But as the message spread further and further afield, the messengers knew that they were not simply telling a remarkable story of things that happened long ago. In particular they were not simply telling a story about a man who rose from the dead—a story that could be classed with other stories of the same kind, with other 'wonders' of the world. In every generation, in every country, this story, this witness, has become contemporary. Today, as then, it is constantly controverted and discussed. Today, as at the beginning, it calls for a total inner commitment. And today it still challenges men to make an absolute surrender which is without a parallel. *That* is what this story means. And it all began in this small, insignificant way, at that particular moment. It is an astonishing fact that something so small as a story, and something so vulnerable as the narrative of an eyewitness, should have had such amazing results. And it is this testimony, the ever-widening circle of those to whom this story was told, which is the final, and also the strongest, weapon in the Church's armoury. Again and again there have been times when all other means of existence were taken from her, and she lived only upon the fact that a few people could not stop telling this story of the Resurrection of Christ wherever they went. And when the Church has been thrown back upon this ultimate weapon, it has always been a great period in her history. Then it has been proved that she cannot be defeated; and it is there that the most distinctive results of this story have been revealed.

Many other events in the life of the Church may be copied by the world. But *this* cannot be copied; it is unique; it can never be repeated. The Church alone possesses this treasure, and she only possesses it because, although she may be poor, defenceless and weak, she still goes on telling this story. It is of course true that people will remind us that there have been forced conversions by fire and sword, for instance among the inhabitants of ancient Germany, but this does not alter the fact that the real cause of the growth of the Church was the 'folly' of its message. It is the influence of the Christian message which has transformed the West. We do not know what to wonder at more: that such a small matter should have such great results, or that such a great matter as the Resurrection from the dead should produce an immediate effect which seemed so futile as this commission: simply, to bear witness. There He stands, Whom the disciples had seen hanging powerless and dying on the Cross—there He stands, alive, before them. In every possible way He has proved that it is He Himself.

And now, they might have thought, now that He has shown that He cannot be overcome, *now* there will be a triumphal progress throughout the world. Now—they might have thought—He will use the powers which have brought Him back to life. Now He will conquer the whole world for Himself, in the twinkling of an eye. Now the great transformation, the resurrection of the world, will be achieved. That is what we *might* have thought, but nothing like this happened. Now, just as before His Crucifixion, He refrains from any extensive use of His power. He comes to His disciples and instead of telling them to go out and prove his Resurrection to all nations, with Himself at their head, He only tells them to spread the story, and then once more He vanishes from their sight. He leaves them defenceless, in face of all the assaults of this world. He leaves His Resurrection as a very disputable fact; He promises to help them, it is true, but evidently this help will come wholly from the unseen world.

All this is most amazing, and the whole history of the Church, which has continued ever since, has therefore also been amazing, because it was a Church which was equipped with nothing more than these defenceless witnesses. Very often the Church was not content with this. Often she did not understand that this alone was sufficient. Often she tried to achieve her mission by other means—and then she was continually thrown back on herself until she realised there was only one thing to do: that she *must* bear witness. We may say—and the first disciples will, I suppose, have felt this—

that it was an act of grace that this victory-march of the Risen Lord, with His visible power, all over the earth, did not take place, that the triumphal procession of Christ only begins to take place in the weak and lowly form of witness. All of you who perhaps have sometimes wished that Christ would manifest more of His Resurrection—be glad that He does not do it, be glad that He makes everything turn upon witness! For that means the same for us all, exactly what it meant at that time to the disciples. They are to begin at Jerusalem, says Christ, and that simply means that Jerusalem which had killed the Messiah is still granted time, time for repentance, time for forgiveness, a fresh offer from God. That is why Christ restrains the exercise of His power, that is why He only allows this witness to go all over the world—in order that there may be time for us all to hear, and listen, and respond, and prepare ourselves for the day when we shall see Him coming in power and great glory.[1]

Now, my friends, when you reach home, and you read through this long passage once more—and I ask you very seriously to do this—you will notice that it contains all the elements which are important for witness—bearing: (i) the 'power from on high', which is mentioned at the close; (ii) that they will *see* something; and (iii) that the Scriptures will be 'opened' to them. Now they must wait for their equipment. This demonstrates for all time that, if the telling of this story is to have such wonderful effects, it cannot possibly happen unless something very special is given from above. If the 'power from on high' is lacking, then this story simply remains an interesting narrative, interesting for historians, but with no effect on real life. Hence, when any one of us proclaims this message—and we are *all* called to be heralds of the Gospel—today or tomorrow, in some conversation or another, we must be both very confident and very humble. We must remember this 'power from on high', on which our whole

---

[1] The 'Confessing Church' was formed in 1933 in order to confess Christ in Hitler's Germany (*Translator*).

strength depends. Then we will become very confident, for we know that with this power the narration of the story and the words of witness may produce amazing results. Where else is there a message, in earth or in heaven, which conquers death? Where else is there a message which draws men out of the deep darkness of the knowledge of sin, into great joy? Where else a message which can really heal a wounded heart, can really comfort a sorrowful person, and can make a dying person sure of eternal life? At the same time the messenger is humble, because he knows that none of this power is in himself. To his humiliation it will be withheld at the very moment when he feels sure of himself; and for his comfort it can happen when, as he sees later, he thought he was quite poor and empty. Everyone who is allowed to bear witness to Someone else, to the life of Jesus Christ, must do it thus: very humbly, but very confidently.[2]

The second point is this: that the witness of the apostles, and of all those who succeeded them, is based upon the testimony of eyewitnesses. That is why we all study the New Testament. That is why we are bound to those men whom we call apostles, because they have *seen* something. Witness to Jesus Christ presupposes that here upon earth something was visible. Because Jesus knows this, He renders them a service before He takes them into His service. He serves them, in showing Himself to them, so that they see Him with their bodily eyes, they touch Him with their own fingers, in order that in future no one may imagine that the Resurrection is only something symbolical or spiritual, only a heavenly and other-worldly reality. The Resurrection *is* a heavenly reality, but at the same time it is also wholly a reality of this world, as we see it in this incident, when Jesus says to His friends: 'Handle Me and see!' In the future, wherever a Christian bears witness, he will not first of all speak about his own inner ex-

[2] For the preacher's subsequent evangelism in the German army and in the heart of Soviet Russia, see his book *Unwilling Journey* (SCM Press, 1953) (*Translator*).

perience. The apostles say very little, but what they do say is enough : they proclaim the news of this fundamental event. So the Church was never again what she had been on Golgotha. Never again did she endure such doubts about God's promises. Never again was her faith assailed in the same way. Through the death of Jesus, through the extremity of loss and of pain, the disciples had experienced the greatest confirmation of all their hopes. The apostles are men who have experienced at the same time both promise and fulfilment. And now, in the future, they proclaim to us all, that—although the fulfilment may have to be delayed for a long time yet—this union of promise and fulfilment is quite certain in the Resurrection of Jesus Christ : there is no promise of God which He will not really fulfil. That is why again and again we gaze at what the apostles are here allowed to see. We do this in order to overcome our temptations, to console ourselves during the time of waiting, and to strengthen our faith. That is why the apostles are the foundations of our faith (Eph. 2.20). On this we build our life today, on something that took place long ago, when, out of extreme distress, there issued the greatest blessing. When everything seemed to be in ruins hope arose, and the mighty fulfilment of God's promise. It is on this that we live today.

And now there comes a third point : the Bible is a book in which, when we read it with care, we are continually confronted by the strangest things. This story which we are now reading seems to me to belong to those which are most unexpected. What would you have done if you had suddenly seen in your midst the One whom you had seen die before your eyes, and Whom you believed to be God's Messenger? Would you not have pelted Him with questions : 'Where have You come from? What was it like in that unknown land from which You come?' Would you not have felt urged to ask about those things which Jesus mentions in the Parable of the Rich Man and Lazarus, and what the man asked for his brothers : a record of conditions in the other world?

But here there is nothing of that kind, and the many questions which we would all have liked to put to Jesus—these interesting, but also difficult and really serious questions—remain unanswered. What does the Lord do, after He has come back to His disciples from the land of death? What is it that *He* regards as the most important thing to do? He gives them a Bible lesson. He gives them a Bible lesson—and seems to think this is the most urgent thing that should happen now. 'Then He opened their minds to understand the scriptures.' That means, that the event, of which they are now eye-witnesses, was a clue to something larger. What they have seen, this Man, Jesus of Nazareth, His working in the name of God and the way in which He has gone through the most profound suffering into the glory of the Resurrection—this is a key, an event which is a revelation through which all the words which God has hitherto spoken, become clear. We need this key in order to be able to read the Old Testament. And if anyone is wondering about the meaning of the Old Testament, he ought to have a great longing that Jesus would come into Him and now as then open up the Old Testament, verse by verse, and show him what no one, apart from Him, can see: that everywhere in the Old Testament the coming of Christ, the sufferings of Christ, and the final victory of God through the midst of suffering, are foretold.

How could anyone possibly hit upon the wrong idea that the Church could do without the Old Testament, even for a day, when Jesus Christ, after His Resurrection, had nothing more important to do than to open the Old Testament and to expound its meaning? How could anyone even think that it is still the Church of Christ if it closes the Old Testament instead of opening it? How is it possible for people to think that we become more Christian, that we can witness to Christ better, if we break with the Old Testament? We look back to that hour and rejoice that this Old Testament has been given to us, and that we may have the conviction that the Man Who opens up to us the hidden mysteries of the Old Testament will one day open up to you and me the hidden mysteries of all human life, of the whole story of your own life. He has the book with the seven seals in His hand. He is worthy to open the book (Rev. 5.9). 'The Lamb who was slain' is the Prince, the Risen Lord.

Luke 24.50-53

Then He led them out as far as Bethany, and lifting up His hands He blessed them. While He blessed them, He parted from them.

And they returned to Jerusalem with great joy, and were continually in the temple blessing God.

W E only begin to see that this conclusion of the Gospel of Luke is very wonderful, when it also begins to dawn upon us that this conclusion is, after all, very strange.

This is the situation: if we have read this Gospel right through, we have reached the end of a very beautiful book, a book which is, indeed, incredibly beautiful. We close it with that kind of regret which we feel when we come to the end of a book which has taken us into a wonderful world—we feel that it, like everything else upon earth, is over, and there is an end of it. We feel rather forsaken, and realise that once more we are back in this world of ours, in our own city, in this year 1940, and in our own life.[1] We wish we could ask the apostles how it was that when, for them too, a book was closed, they evidently did not feel this regret. For why did they speak of the great joy which filled their hearts? Surely they were now forsaken, just as we are—now that their time of vision was over, and the hard task of faith seemed to have

[1] The preacher feared that this would be one of his last sermons to the congregation (*Translator*).

begun? Now surely they were once more orphans, and indeed in addition, members of a forsaken Church, a Church which had lost its Shepherd and had been told that it would find itself in the world like a scattered flock of sheep who have fallen among wolves. The most terrible things were said to be going to happen to them, and yet they were full of 'great joy'. 'They were continually in the Temple, blessing God.' That is how the Gospel of Luke ends.

This can only be due to the fact that these men knew for certain something about which so many of us are uncertain. Evidently, they knew at once that this 'departure' of Christ was final; they knew at once that this was the last time that they would see Him upon this earth; they knew that He had not gone away from them in order to come back to them in a new way, as He had been doing. They knew that this period of His bodily manifestations were over. But they knew, too, that—in another sense—it was not final. This was not the end of a brief visit to this earth. When they saw Him no more it would not seem like a beautiful dream from which they had awakened to harsh reality. No, they knew that now God's presence with them in a new way was just beginning.

Luke, the Evangelist who links the Book of the Acts of the Apostles directly with the Gospel, is not aiming at giving us first of all a record of the deeds of Christ, for which we praise God, and then a record of the deeds of some particular people —as though after the life of Christ it would be worth while describing any human life. No, his aim is to continue the story of the deeds of Christ, of the exalted Christ, and to praise Him for them. That is why Luke wrote the Acts of the Apostles. It was in order to impress upon all the Christian communities who would read it that here nothing has come to an end. God has not begun a mighty work and then broken it off midway. God does not break off His history; He leads it on to its consummation, to the glory for which He has planned it.

That is the certainty which fills them with such joy: it is

going on, right into the future. This joy has two elements. On the one hand, they know that this is a parting—yet, on the other, they know that He is present. It is true that He was 'carried up', as we read in the Greek text—but He remains here. It is true that something has come to an end—but it is only the beginning which has ended, and now what Christ began is going further. It is true, that so far as this earth is concerned, nothing seems to have changed; the whole world does not know what has taken place; it goes on living its old life as though nothing had happened; it still has its wars; it worships its gods; it allows its old gods to be overthrown and it invents new ones; it loves and it hates; its life goes on as before, whether in joy or sorrow. But in the midst of all this a divine history has begun, and it does not stop, but it is still going on, and it is the sign of hope for the whole darkened world. It is a light which shines in the darkness and it will never be put out. It is a proclamation that a day will come when the night will be over for good, and so through the apparent sorrow of 'departure' there will break the dawn of joy.

Ascension Day is not a minor festival. People who are perplexed by the wonder of this Ascension of Christ, and who would rather not think of it in the physical sense, should note that to follow this line of thought closes the way to joy. This does not mean, of course, that 'He was carried up into heaven' was something that could be observed with their human eyes. Probably it is a phrase inserted into the Gospel later on—some manuscripts, the most ancient ones, do not contain it—and the scribe who added it probably did not mean that this was what the apostles saw with their bodily eyes, but rather that this was something which they now knew by faith, namely, that He who suddenly disappeared is now 'sitting at the right hand of God the Father', and 'heaven has received Him'. Why is this so important? Because—and this is why the apostles are so full of joy—heaven and earth are now linked by an inseparable bond. The Ascension does *not* mean that Christ is

119

separated from this world. Because He returns to the Father as the Incarnate Son, because He has not laid aside the body as a butterfly leaves the chrysalis behind, because as Man He 'parted from them'—because of this, the Church has been so sure that now God will never leave this world to itself, He will never let it go. Now the world of God and the world of Man will never more be separated. Now that which is 'above' is no longer something quite foreign, supernatural, but He Whom we know, Whom our Christmas hymns call our 'Brother', He Who has assumed our human nature, our very being, Who shares our life, now stands there in the heavenly world; He is now at God's right hand. The early Church theologians coined the final phrase for this: *Quod unquam assumpsit, nunquam deponit*, 'That which He once assumed He never again lays down.'

Now can you see that this is the reason for 'great joy'? There would be no certainty for this earth, no hope at all, were there not this inseparable link between earth and heaven. You should reflect upon this, and be quite sure that this does not merely mean the world in general, but that this link is forged with your present life, here and now, upon this earth. So when you read a word of judgment in the Scriptures, when you begin to feel anxious and troubled in an hour of great distress about your own sins, of the hopelessness towards which you are going, then know this: that there, above, at the right hand of God the Father, sits One Who is no other than the Brother Who knows your life from within, Who has united you to Himself, and equally with the life of us all, especially of those about whom we are anxious. The *Lord* is our *Brother*.

Full of joy, then, the apostles went back to the city, and stayed in the Temple, and joined the waiting community of the Old Testament. Luke the Evangelist knows why he lays so much stress on the fact that this takes place in the *Temple*. These men are not revolutionaries; they are not throwing off the old; they do not think, as every revolutionary thinks, that history begins with them, and only then begins to have a meaning. They link themselves with those who went before them, and although they are persecuted by their own people, and stigmatised as traitors by the chief priests, they claim that they have received the true meaning of the great promises of the Old Testament. There is nothing greater in world history before the Birth of Christ than the fact that in the Old Dispensation a few people waited and hoped and saw a great light bringing salvation to the world. And now it has come— and they have still not ceased to wait. Now the fulfilment is here—and yet they look for the promise. Now the end of the world is here—and the world still exists and 'lies in the evil one.' So they stand, radiant in the light of fulfilment—and yet still at the point where they wait for the promise, as do we all. We could not expect Christ if we could not expect Him with the people of Israel, with the Old Testament, if we were not to look for Him in union with men of hope in the Old Testament.

Some manuscripts here have a wrong reading in this passage. They read: 'After He had blessed them He parted from them.' The most ancient manuscripts read: 'While He passage. They read: 'After He had blessed them He parted from them! When someone leaves us we constantly recall in our memory the last gesture and the last expression on his face and we cannot forget it. And the last that the Church sees of her Lord is that He is in the act of blessing her! The gesture of blessing does not cease; it lasts on into eternity. It fills this period between the Ascension and the Return of Christ. What is He doing now? He is blessing us. This blessing means: His gift of power, the assurance of His return, the fulfilment of all the promises of God, and the establishment of the Christian brotherhood. When the blessing is pronounced at the close of a service of worship, we may be sure of this: that for these two thousand years Christ has been, and still is, blessing His Church. She lives by the power of this blessing all down the centuries, to the present day. The

Church is like a slender reed in the wind, and her faith is like a feeble flickering wick. Long ago all would have been extinguished—if He had not gone on blessing her. Some of us here may feel envious of the joy of these disciples and of their certainty. Perhaps we feel 'poor' alongside of this joy of the Primitive Church, and it is indeed true that Christendom, and in it our own Church, has fallen into a state of great and culpable poverty. The remnant of joy which we do possess however, is still a relic of that great joy with which the Primitive Church so joyfully and victoriously endured all her trials of persecution and loneliness—and overcame. So if any of us feels poor and joyless compared with such 'great joy', we may remind ourselves that even if the light within us is only burning feebly and uncertainly, and our faith seems to be more like a tiny flickering candle, yet we may still be glad that in the fellowship of the Church this great joy was, and still is, present, breaking out over and over again. Indeed we are in the fellowship of the Church precisely because where one of us is poor, another brother is rich in faith. In our own congregation we may well pray that among the many who are 'poor' there may be a few who are full of certainty and joy.

'And they were continually in the Temple, blessing God.' So the Gospel ends. 'And they were praising God,' writes Luke the Evangelist in the Acts of the Apostles about that night when Paul and Silas were in prison at Philippi (Acts 16.25). 'They were praying and singing hymns to God.' When this happened something had begun to take place which for two thousand years or more the world had never known. The world fears its gods; it respects them, but in fear; it never sings praises to them. And if anyone thinks he does not need this Gospel, then we may ask him whether he is a man who, without this story of Jesus Christ, can really continually 'praise God'. And as we ask this question, let us hasten with the shepherds to Bethlehem and join with the band of those who are praising God. Henceforth this is the one thing that matters. Whatever the world may look like one thing stands firm : this one event will continually be to us a cause for ever-renewed thanks and praise, so that at the end of our life, when we are about to enter into His kingdom, it will become absolutely clear to us. For what end were we created? To praise God. What will fill our eternal life? The praise of God. What then is the only thing permanent in our earthly life? . . . 'They praised God.'